Merton of th

Movies

IN FOUR ACTS

A DRAMATIZATION OF HARRY LEON WILSON'S STORY OF THE SAME NAME

By George S. Kaufman and Marc Connelly

SAMUEL FRENCH, INC.
25 WEST 45TH STREET   NEW YORK 10036
7623 SUNSET BOULEVARD   HOLLYWOOD 90046
LONDON   TORONTO

The following is a copy of the program of the first performance of MERTON OF THE MOVIES, produced at the Cort Theatre, New York City, Monday evening, November 13th, 1922:

MERTON OF THE MOVIES

A Dramatization of Harry Leon Wilson's story of the same name

By

GEORGE S. KAUFMAN AND MARC CONNELLY

(Direction of George C. Tyler and Hugh Ford)
Staged by Hugh Ford

THE CAST
(In Order of Appearance)

		Original Cast
MERTON GILL	....	*Glen Hunter*
AMOS G. GASHWILER	....	*Edward M. Favor*
ELMER HUFF	....	*Bert Melville*
TESSIE KEARNS	....	*Esther Pinch*
CASTING DIRECTOR	....	*Lucile Webster*
J. LESTER MONTAGUE	....	*J. K. Murray*
SIGMOND ROSENBLATT	....	*Edwin Maxwell*
WELLER	....	*Tom Hadaway*
HIS CAMERAMAN	....	*Albert Cowles*
THE MONTAGUE GIRL	....	*Florence Nash*
HAROLD PARMALEE	....	*Alexander Clark, Jr.*
BEULAH BAXTER	....	*Gladys Feldman*
MURIEL MERCER	....	*Mary Forbes*
JEFF BAIRD	....	*John Webster*
MRS. PATTERSON	....	*Clara Sidney*
MR. WALBERG	....	*Edwin Maxwell*

SYNOPSIS OF SCENES

ACT I

Gashwiler's General Store, Simsbury, Illinois.
A Saturday Night.

ACT II

Outside the Holden Lot, Hollywood.

ACT III

On the Lot.

SCENE I: Stage No. 6.
SCENE II: Stage No. 6.   Tank Set.   A week later.

ACT IV

SCENE I: Jeff Baird's Office.   A few weeks later.
SCENE II: Merton's Rooming House.

MERTON OF THE MOVIES

ACT I

SCENE: *The rear of the Gashwiler General Store.
Ten o'clock on a Saturday night. Up stage a
counter, with shelves behind it, runs across
stage to a door L. of C. From a point L. of the
door, another counter runs down stage. A window overlooks the latter from the height of
eight or nine feet. Down right is another counter or the end of one. The effect is that the
street entrance is somewhere off right.* MER-
TON'S *bed and trunk are concealed in the counter down* R. *Phonograph on counter at* R.

AT RISE: GASHWILER *back of counter, busy.* EL-
MER *enters* R., *sees* GASHWILER—*starts to exit,
as* GASHWILER *speaks.*

GASHWILER. *(None too pleased to see him)* How
are you, Elmer?
ELMER. *(Not meeting* GASHWILER'S *eye)* I'm
—all right, I guess. *(Pause.)* How are *you*, Mr.
Gashwiler?
GASHWILER. I don't change much.
ELMER. *(Agreeing with him a little too enthusi-
astically)* That's right. *(An awkward pause.)* It's
getting—late, isn't it?

5

GASHWILER. M'm.

ELMER. Guess you'll be closing up pretty soon.

GASHWILER. M'm. *(Puts book away—a pause.)* There's still time, though, Elmer, if you want to buy something.

ELMER. Huh? Oh, no, thanks.—I wasn't thinking of that. *(Another awkward pause.)* Is—ah— is Mrs. Gashwiler all right? *(Takes hat off.)*

GASHWILER. I suppose you want to see Merton?

ELMER. Well, as long as I'm here, I did think I'd drop in on him. *(Puts cane, then hat, on table right.)*

GASHWILER. *(Comes from back of counter to* ELMER, R.C.—*seriously)* Elmer? *(Looks off, coming down.)*

ELMER. Yes, sir.

GASHWILER. I—I don't want you to get Merton in no bad habits.

ELMER. Me?—why——

GASHWILER. Now hold on. I don't mean this personal—exactly—but Merton's different from most of you boys. He's—funny, sort of. But he's got the makings of a fine boy, and I don't want to see him get started *wrong*.

ELMER. I'm not going to do anything to him. *(Sits on edge of table.)*

GASHWILER. You see, it ain't as though he had any parents—I been sort of looking after him ever since he came to work here. *(Looks off* L. ELMER *follows.)* Besides, if he goes out nights, he ain't no good in the store mornings.

ELMER. But honest, Mr. Gashwiler, I'm only going to *talk* to him.

GASHWILER. I wish I knew what you and him talk about all the time. *(Gets cigar—goes back to counter.)* Merton's been awful dreamy lately—can't keep his mind on things a bit.

ELMER. *(To counter)* It ain't me, Mr. Gashwiler. I can't get him to come out with us or noth-ing. *(Crossing* R.*)*

GASHWILER. Oh, then you *do try?*

ELMER. *(Trapped)* Well—well, anyhow, he *won't.*

GASHWILER. You're telling me—the truth, El-mer?

ELMER. *(Turns to* GASHWILER*)* Yes, sir. Why, he hasn't even played poker with us for months. *(Sits on box.)* He don't go anywhere—— *(He remembers that this is not strictly true)*—except—— *(He stops, rather abruptly.)*

GASHWILER. *(Slowly)* Yes. I know what you're going to say. *(He looks off* L.*, then turns back again.)* Moving pictures.

ELMER. Yes, sir. That's all he'll talk about to *anybody.*

GASHWILER. I hope they ain't going to his head. Merton's an awful sensitive boy.

ELMER. Just the same, he goes to them all the time, Mr. Gashwiler, and I think you ought to know it. Why, he—he imitates the *people* in 'em, too.

GASHWILER. I don't know what he's coming to. *(He looks around to see if* MERTON *is coming; then brings up a magazine from under the counter.)* I—I found this underneath the counter a while ago. Know what it is?

ELMER. *(Goes up to counter to* GASHWILER— *reading the title)* "Cameraland." It's a moving pic-ture magazine.

GASHWILER. Yes, I know it is. *(He turns a few pages, idly.)* Even got magazines about 'em. Got a lot of pictures in it about bungalows and—Japanese hired help. I hope Merton don't get all worked up by it. *(Puts it away.)*

ELMER. Charley Harper seen him down in Ford's meadow at five o'clock yesterday morning. He **had** your horse there.

GASHWILER. My Dexter? *(Comes to* ELMER.)

ELMER. Yes, sir.

GASHWILER. Are you *sure?*

ELMER. Pretty sure. Lem Hardy was there with his picture camera, and Merton had his arm around the horse's neck one time, and was talking to it.

GASHWILER. Did Charley hear what he said?

ELMER. He wasn't close enough. At first he didn't know what to make of it, and then he remembered there'd been a William S. Hart picture at the Bijou Palace the night before.

GASHWILER. You mean—Merton was *imitating* him? *(Looks down* L.)

ELMER. That's what.

GASHWILER. You think—he might want to be a picture actor?

ELMER. It certainly looks like it.

(GASHWILER *hesitates a second and then crosses determinedly to* L.)

GASHWILER. Merton! *(Pause.)* Merton!

MERTON. *(Off)* Yes, sir.

GASHWILER. Leave off whatever you're doing and look here a minute.

MERTON. *(Off)* Yes, sir. *(He enters left.)* Oh, hello, Elmer.

ELMER. *(Uneasily)* 'Lo, Merton. *(Rising from counter—goes to* R.)

MERTON. *(To* GASHWILER) It's—ten o'clock.

GASHWILER. You can close up in a minute. First I want to ask you a question.

MERTON. Yes, sir.

GASHWILER. Was it you down in the meadow—yesterday morning?

MERTON. *(With a quick glance at* ELMER) Yes, sir. *(Puts basket on counter.)*

GASHWILER. With—the horse, *again?*

MERTON. Yes, sir.

GASHWILER. You couldn't have been—hitching him up—before six—could you?

MERTON. No—sir, I just—wanted to see if he was all right. *(R.)*

GASHWILER. I don't know as I understand you lately—Merton.

MERTON. I'm—just the same. *(Crosses R. to close door.)*

GASHWILER. No, you ain't—you're different. *(Pause.)* And I know what it is.

MERTON. It's not anything.

GASHWILER. Yes, it is. It's moving pictures. You just keep on working steady and you'll get there much faster than if you was always running out to picture shows.

MERTON. Yes, sir.

GASHWILER. Here! Here's your money. *(Handing him three five-dollar bills. Coming down.)*

MERTON. Thank you.

GASHWILER. Hope you're saving it. *(ELMER rises.)*

MERTON. *(To counter L.)* Well, I can't save the whole fifteen, each week.

GASHWILDER. If you wasn't so flighty, I'd say you had the makin's of a wealthy man.

MERTON. I don't think I'm flighty. *(Crosses R.)*

GASHWILER. Well, you seem to moon around a lot. You're not going out, are you?

MERTON. No, sir.

GASHWILER. That's good. *(Taps.)* There's mother tapping for me. Oh—when you lock up, don't forget to bring them new dummies back here. I don't want no sunlight to get on them and ruin 'em tomorrow.

MERTON. Yes, sir.

GASHWILER. Well, I'm going to bed. Goodnight.

MERTON.   Good-night!

GASHWILER.   *(Looks up at window)*   Don't forget to lock that window.   *(Sharply.)*

MERTON.   No, sir.

GASHWILER.   Don't waste them lamps.

MERTON.   *(After a look that should wither)*   No, sir.   (GASHWILER *goes into his office. Crosses* L., *looks after* GASHWILER.)   Where were you—at the pictures?   *(Interested.)*

ELMER.   Me?— No.   (MERTON *turns away.)* How soon'll you be through?

MERTON.   I'm through now except for putting things away.   *(Starts to cover tables.)*

ELMER.   How about a little session with My Lady *Luck?*

MERTON.   No, I can't.   *(At counter* L.)

ELMER.   Oh, why can't you?   Gee whiz, that's the third time this month you've stayed away. *(Pauses.)*   Anything been upsetting you?   Are you sore at anybody?

MERTON.   No!

ELMER.   *(Laughs)*   I thought maybe it was because Dan Turner kidded you about buying that cowboy outfit.

MERTON.   Nobody got me sore about anything. *(He looks at* ELMER.)   That's right, Elmer, I'm not sore.

ELMER.   Then what's the reason you don't meet up with the crowd any more?   I'd think you'd want *some* relaxation.

MERTON.   Well, I'll put it frankly to you, Elmer. I can't afford to run around with the crowd.   I've got other *interests.*

ELMER.   *What other interests?*

MERTON.   Well, I have them . . . that's all.

ELMER.   *(Nearer to* MERTON)   You're not in love with some girl?

MERTON. *(With a bit of disgust)* Is that what they think?

ELMER. No, but—— *(Confidentially)* Is that it, Merton? Are you in love with some girl?

MERTON. Why, how rid—— *(He is about to say "ridiculous" when a realization of the truth makes him change his statement.)* Well, maybe I *am,* in a way.

ELMER. Who *is* she?

MERTON. *(Dramatizing it)* I don't think you have the honor of her acquaintance, Elmer.

ELMER. *(Concerned only in the news)* Where does she live?

MERTON. In a place far away.

ELMER. *(Laughs)* Oh—— Where did *you* ever meet anybody in a place far away? You've never *been* anywhere's—except like when you went to Peoria last month. *(MERTON gives him a quick look.)*

MERTON. She could be a *visitor* here in Simsbury, *couldn't she?*

ELMER. *(Giving it quite a lot of thought)* No, *she couldn't!* I've seen everybody that ever visited here. *(Suddenly)* It ain't that girl that come over from Masonville to help at the restaurant. She's terrible. Why, she's——

MERTON. *(Stopping him by a gesture)* That isn't the person. Really, you don't know her. And as for this lady being a mere restaurant girl—why, she's on a mountain peak!

ELMER. *(Affected by MERTON's air)* Oh, boy!

MERTON. *(Reprovingly)* This thing's all pretty sacred to me, Elmer. *(Up to door L.)*

ELMER. Well, it's your funeral. But I certainly think a man ought to have a *little* amusement. Here—— *(He extends cigarettes.)*

MERTON. No, thanks, Elmer. *(Crosses to counter.)*

ELMER. Don't you even *smoke* any more?

MERTON. No. *(He turns away from adjusting the last cover on counter.)* I guess you think I must be nutty, don't you, Elmer?

ELMER. No, I don't, no matter *what* people say.

MERTON. How do you mean—what they say?

ELMER. Oh, about—things you do. You can trust *me*, Merton—tell me, *were* you in the pasture this morning, talking to the horse?

MERTON. What horse?

ELMER. Gashwiler's horse. Charlie Harper said he saw you with your arms around his neck.

MERTON. What would I be talking to a horse for? *(Crosses R.)*

ELMER. Of course, I can understand—I mean, if you were—*lonesome.*

MERTON. It isn't—that—I never said I was—— *(Knock on door. To* ELMER*)* It's Tessie Kearns. *(Crosses to door* R.I.*)* Hello!

(Enter MISS KEARNS.*)*

MISS KEARNS. Hello, Merton. I thought I'd come and tell you about the picture.

MERTON. Thanks.

*(*MISS KEARNS *carries a movie magazine and an envelope containing photographs.)*

MISS KEARNS. Good evening, Elmer.

ELMER. *(Without much cordiality)* H'llo, Miss Kearns. *(To* MERTON*)* Well, I guess I'll meander—— *(Crosses* R. *to door.)*

MISS KEARNS. *(*C.*)* I hope I'm not interrupting you, gentlemen!

MERTON. *(Quickly)* Oh, no!

ELMER. *(In the same breath)* We were just talking. I gotta get down to a *meeting,* anyway. Sorry you can't come, Mert. G'night, Miss Kearns.

G'night, Mert. (ELMER *exits as* MERTON *murmurs a good-night.*)

MISS KEARNS.   Are you sure I didn't *interrupt?*

MERTON.   *(Crosses to* TESSIE, *front of counter)* No, I was glad you come.   I want to hear about the picture.   He only wanted me to go to a poker game.

MISS KEARNS.   *(Politely)*   Maybe you wanted to go.

MERTON.   No!   You see, with me it's either idle pleasure or a career, and I'm going to have the career.   Was the picture good to-night?

MISS KEARNS.   It was great!   Oh, here are some prints Mr. Hardy, the photographer, asked me to give you.—I nearly forgot.

MERTON.   Thanks.   *(Up behind table to* C.—*takes them consciously.)*   You know what they are?

MISS KEARNS.   You, ain't they?

MERTON.   *(Trying to pass it off lightly)*   They're —*stills* of me—in different characters.

MISS KEARNS.   *(Rises)*   Oh, Merton!   Can I see them?

MERTON.   Would you really like to?

MISS KEARNS.   I'd be delighted.   *(Sits.* MERTON *starts to open the envelope.)*   And oh, yes!   Mr. Hardy said to tell you he'd meet you at two-thirty to-morrow, just as you said.

MERTON.   *(Casually)*   On the Lot.

MISS KEARNS.   *(Awed by this technical knowledge)*   Uh-huh.

MERTON.   He's—— *(Handing her a photograph)*—a great help to a man like me who is studying.

MISS KEARNS.   Oh, this is fine!   You look wonderful in evening dress.   Merton, why, you just seem to be an actor already.

MERTON.   *(Abandoning the consideration of the photograph in his hand to go over and examine the one he has given* MISS KEARNS.)   That's a society man type. *(He draws back a pace and looks at it from a distance.)* Notice anything particular about it?

MISS KEARNS. *(After a moment)* Well, you look very refined and dignified.

MERTON. No, I mean the face.

MISS KEARNS. *(Doing her best to find something)* Why, ah——

MERTON. Wait. *(He crosses to the counter down L. and throws back the curtain that has masked a cot, a small trunk and two or three boxes beneath the counter from the view of the audience. From one of the boxes he takes out a photograph and carries it to MISS KEARNS.)* Know who that is?

MISS KEARNS. Harold Parmalee! A wonderful artist.

MERTON. Perhaps the greatest star in a certain type of part the screen will ever see. *(He holds it beside the photograph of himself, which MISS KEARNS holds.)* Now do you notice anything?

MISS KEARNS. *(Looks at him. Rises, back to R.C.—amazed)* Yes, sir! You do! You do! With that *suit* and everything—— *(Crosses MERTON to L.C.)* It's really remarkable. I don't know that your shoulders are quite—— *(This hurts. He almost grabs the picture.)*

MERTON. No, I know they're not. Of course, I don't intend to imitate him, anyway. When I begin acting professionally, I intend creating my own particular types. *(Spreads photos on table.)*

MISS KEARNS. Have you made up your mind yet when you're going?

MERTON. *(Back of couch C.)* Pretty soon now. I've got two hundred and seventy dollars. I figure in another month or so I'll have a clear three hundred.

MISS KEARNS. And then you'll go out to California?

MERTON. The minute I get three hundred. *(He crosses L. to* TESSIE.) I've got about all the clothes I need now. They can't say I haven't the equipment. I've got Western suits, automobile clothes, a suit for polo, everything!

MISS KEARNS. *(Depressed)* I'll be sorry to see you go—in a way, Merton. But I know you're going to be a big success as an actor.

MERTON. Well, I've been working hard at it. But I guess I'm still pretty far from perfect.

MISS KEARNS. Nonsense! You took all that *correspondence course,* didn't you?

MERTON. *(Laughs)* It was funny, my thinking I knew everything before I took that course. Did I show you their certificate? *(Brings it out of pocket.)*

MISS KEARNS. Um! All engraved.

MERTON. You bet.

MISS KEARNS. "Film Incorporation Bureau, Station N, Stebbinsville, Kansas." It's a wonderful name you took, Merton. *(Reads from certificate)* "Clifford Armytage."

MERTON. I picked it myself.

MISS KEARNS. It sounds so real. You're an actor now, all right. *(A pause.)* Only I had no idea you might be going so soon. *(Crosses R. to table.)*

MERTON. Just the minute I get three hundred. *(Steps L.)*

MISS KEARNS. It'll be pretty quiet here.

MERTON. You ought to come out, too, Tessie. That's the place for a scenario writer.

MISS KEARNS. Not on what the millinery business is paying.

MERTON. You know a photo playwright ought to be right on the ground just as much as an actor. All the world-famous authors go out there. Rex Beach, Elinor Glyn, Maeterlinck and Rupert Hughes——

Miss Kearns. But I'm nowhere near world famous. I haven't sold even one story yet.

Merton. You mark my words, you'll sell "Passion's Perils." I'll bet you the Touchstone people take it.

Miss Kearns. No, they won't. I got it back this evening.

Merton. *(Astonished)* Well, they make me sick! But we've both got to be patient. We can't succeed all at once—remember that. *(Crosses R. to Tessie.)*

Miss Kearns. Oh, I'm patient—but I guess we'd both get discouraged sometimes if it wasn't for our sense of humor.

Merton. I know *I* would. If it wasn't for fine artists like Beulah Baxter—— *(He recalls that he has not yet heard about the film.)* You said it was a good instalment tonight, huh?

Miss Kearns. *(Enthusiastic)* M'm! The best yet.

Merton. Just my luck it would come on a Saturday. What happened? *(Crosses to L.C.)*

Miss Kearns. Well, this episode's still up in Alaska.

Merton. I'll bet she was wonderful. What was the menace?

Miss Kearns. They got the cabin surrounded by wolves and then set fire to it. It was harrowing. I don't blame you for admiring her. She's certainly fearless.

Merton. The wonder woman of the silver screen, *I* call her.

Miss Kearns. One time tonight she fought a wolf, hand to hand.

Merton. Gee!

Miss Kearns. I thought for a minute it was a double—it was so—daring.

Merton. Well, you can get *that* idea out of your

head. I told you what she said at that personal appearance in Peoria. She said if she ever used a double in "Hazards of Hortense," why, she'd feel she wasn't keeping faith with her public.

Miss Kearns. It must have been wonderful, being virtually face to face with her.

Merton. It certainly was, and very inspiring. Why, she just *swayed* that audience.

Miss Kearns. Mr. Gashwiler never found out *why* you went up to Peoria, did he?

Merton. No, but if he did I wouldn't hesitate to admit it. Miss Baxter is a great influence in my life. That Elmer Huff got me a little sore just now. *(Crosses L.)*

Miss Kearns. Why, what—what did he do?

Merton. Nothing, really. But Miss Baxter's name almost came up in the course of conversation. If he'd have spoken lightly of her I'd have lost control of myself. *(A pause.)* Say, Tessie, wouldn't it be wonderful if—when I went out there—*(Crosses R. to Tessie)*—I got a chance to work with her in a picture?

Miss Kearns. I hope you do, Merton.

Merton. Gee!

Miss Kearns. Well, I'll be getting along—oh— *(Starts R.—stops.)* You know, Merton, in a way I'm just as glad you didn't see the show tonight. They had another of those comedies.

Merton. Jeff Baird's? She'd be revolted if she knew her work was on the same bill. Here's a wonderful artist, on one hand, trying to do better and finer things all the time, like "Hazards of Hortense," and alongside of her they put a cheap thing like one of those Jeff Baird comedies. Was the cross-eyed man in it again?

Miss Kearns. Yes, he was.

Merton. It's enough to discourage a *real* artist.

Miss Kearns. Still, there were times when I could hardly keep from laughing.

Merton. They oughtn't to allow them to be made.

Miss Kearns. No, I suppose not. *(A pause.)* Well, good-night. *(Gathering up pictures and magazines.)*

Merton. What's that? *(To her. Crosses to* r. *to table.)* "Silver Screenings?"

Miss Kearns. Yes, I've finished with it—if you want it.

Merton. *(Taking it)* Thanks. Corliss Palmer is beautiful, isn't she? *(He starts looking through it quickly.)* Here's an interview with Harold Parmalee! I've got a cap something like that.

Miss Kearns. It's an awful good piece about him. I liked it where he says—— *(She looks at the story to refresh her memory.)* Ah——

Merton. *(Reading)* "Hard work and the constant striving toward an ideal . . ."

Miss Kearns. *(Turns page)* No—here at the *end.*

Merton. Ah! About his *wife!* *(Reads)* "She is not only my best pal, but my severest critic."

Miss Kearns. It's a lovely tribute.

Merton. And to a splendid woman.

Miss Kearns. *(Pause)* Well, I got to be going.

Merton. *(Following her right)* Good-night. Did Mr. Samuels tell you what he was going to show week after next? *(Crosses* r. *to door. Opens door.)*

Miss Kearns. *(Crosses to door, turns)* He wasn't sure yet. *(Turns.)* Probably a return engagement of "A Fool's Paradise." Good-night.

Merton. Good-night, Tessie.

(She exits. He closes door, pulls shades on windows and doors. Then takes dummies over to

L.C. *The female figure wears a checked ging-*
ham dress, with the card: "Our Latest for Mi-
lady: only $6.98." The male dummy wears a
raincoat, and a card reading: "Rainproof or
You Get Your Money Back." The male dummy
has a small, tip-curled black mustache. MER-
TON *places the dummies near the counter which*
runs down the left of the stage. He sneers at
the male dummy.)

MERTON. You cur!

(His mind still on the dummies, he crosses to the
open trunk and takes out a wallet. As he puts
money in it, he notices sombrero near by. He
puts it on with another glance at the dummies.
Crosses to the string regulating the ceiling lamp
and pulls it, dramatically, throwing the room
into virtual darkness, save for the spot about the
small lamp on the counter and the moonlight
pouring in through the window. He climbs onto
counter at stage L. *to close window.)*

MERTON. *(To male dummy—as the Man)* One-
a-little kiss, Senorita.
(As the woman)
  Ah, God in heaven, is there no help at hand!
(MERTON *speaks)*
  Just a minute, my friend.
(To the female dummy, as Buck Benson)
  I trust I am not too late, Miss St. Clair?—Yes, it's
me, Buck Benson, at your service, ma'am. I suppose
this—this gentleman has been annoying you. Oh,
he has, has he? *(Turns to the villain)* Now, curse
you, you shall fight me in American fashion, man to
man! Viper though you are, I hesitate to put a bullet through your craven heart! *(He screams—turns*
to female dummy.) No, you dog! *(Takes off coat.)*

We shall learn whose body goes over yondeɪ cliff. *(He seizes the male dummy and backs him well over the counter at stage* L. *The door opens and* GASH-WILER *enters without coat.* MERTON *lifts the dummy over his head and is apparently about to throw him over the counter when* GASHWILER'S *voice stops him.)*

GASHWILER. Merton Gill, put down that dummy!

MERTON. *(Doing so)* Yes, sir.

GASHWILER. What do you think you're doin', anyway? Sounded upstairs like riotin'. Suppose you think I got them things down from Chicago just for you to play horse with. Where do you think you are? Actin' in grand op'ry? *(He is examining the male figure for possible damage.)*

MERTON. I didn't do it any harm.

GASHWILER. Maybe you didn't and maybe you did. How'd you like me to lift *you* up and throw you over that counter?

MERTON. I'm sorry.

GASHWILER. I declare, Merton, I don't know what to make of you. If you had a father or mother you'd certainly be a trial. What are you wearin' that big hat for?

MERTON. It's part of a costume. *(Crosses* L., *puts hat and belt in trunk.)*

GASHWILER. You look like a cowboy. You ain't tryin' to *be* a cowboy?

MERTON. I might.

GASHWILER. Well, you can't be one around here. I swear I think you go to them movies too much. They're not the right thing for a feller that's got your nature. You're too hysterical.

MERTON. I go to them to study, Mr. Gashwiler, and I certainly don't intend to stop.

GASHWILER. Jest what do you mean—study?

MERTON. Well, I may as well tell you—I'm studying the movies, with the idea of going into them.

GASHWILER. Actin'?

MERTON. Yes, sir.

GASHWILER. *(Astounded)* My God, you are crazy! Well, let me tell you this, young man! I don't want any more studyin' while you're workin' for me.

MERTON. You don't mean that, do you, Mr. Gashwiler?

GASHWILER. *I certainly do. . . .* There's a limit, Merton. I can't afford havin' anybody around whose spare time ain't spent in something worth while.

MERTON. And you don't think motion pictures are?

GASHWILER. I certainly do not.

MERTON. Well, then, I'll leave, Mr. Gashwiler, right now.

GASHWILER. You'll what?

MERTON. I'll leave. I'm going out to California and—enter the films. I was going anyhow—in a month—but I'll go right away.

GASHWILER. To—to California?

MERTON. Yes, sir.

GASHWILER. To be an actor?

MERTON. Yes, sir, and I'll succeed, too.

GASHWILER. *(Steps R.)* 'Tain't likely—a boy from Simsbury.

MERTON. Lincoln walked four miles for a book.

GASHWILER. Yes, but you ain't studying for President. You're trying to get into something that nobody I ever heard of succeeded in.

MERTON. Well, just the same, Mr. Gashwiler, I'm going to *follow my star.*

GASHWILER. All right, Merton, if that's what you

want to do, then I'm to go right ahead—and—get somebody else?

MERTON. *(Pause)* Yes, sir. *(Crosses* L.)

GASHWILER. You got much money?

MERTON. Two hundred and seventy dollars.

GASHWILER. *(Almost gets money out of pocket, changes his mind)* Well, I . . . I hope you make a big success of it, Merton. Good-night!

MERTON. Good-night, Mr. Gashwiler, and I'm sorry about the dummies.

GASHWILER. That's all right. You didn't hurt them none. *(Looks at* MERTON.) I can't just make you out, Merton. You're a nice boy, one of the nicest I ever knew, but I guess you're just crazy. *(Exits up* C.)

(MERTON *looks after him for a second, then moves male dummy to* L.C., *then starts the phonograph. It is a Walter Camp Daily Dozen record. He follows the instructions of the voice from the phonograph: "Hands on hips, bend trunk forward to angle of forty-five degrees; now back; forward; back," etc. Then gradually he stops exercising, and talks through the phonograph to the male dummy.)*

MERTON. Some day we shall meet again. *(Phonograph)* This time your life has been spared. *(Another pause;* MERTON *changes his tactics and begins to address an imaginary interviewer.)* You ask me to tell the readers of your magazine to what I owe my success? Hard work, young lady. Hard work and the constant striving toward an ideal to give the best that is in me to my public. Perhaps I owe most, however, to Mrs. Armytage, my wife. She is more than a wife. She is my best pal, and, I may say, my severest critic. *(Clock is heard ticking. He stops the machine and blows out the lamp lights. He pulls the cot from under the counter into the moonlight. He kneels beside it.)* Oh, God, make me a good movie actor! Make me one of the best. For Jesus' sake, amen!

CURTAIN

ACT II

Time: *Three weeks after Act I.*

Scene: *The waiting-room outside the Holden lot
in Los Angeles. It is nearly rectangular and
quite bare. There are two doors—one at the
left that leads to and from the outside world,
and one at the right that leads on into the mysteries of the lot. On this latter door is a sign:
"No Admittance Except on Order." The rec-
tangle of the room is broken only by a small
window in the upper right corner—and over it
the words, "Casting Director." On a ledge just
inside this window is a telephone, and through
the window can also be seen a sparsely furnished
office. As for the reception room itself, its floor
is bare, and its walls, of some dull-toned and un-
inspiring stuff, are almost so. A bare bench
runs the length of the rear wall. There is a sign
on the wall: "Attention, Artistes! Costumes
Should Be Returned Promptly to the Wardrobe
Room. Not Responsible for Damage to Wardrobe Furnished by Artistes. Talent Checks
Should Be Cashed Promptly. Report Changes
of Address or Telephone Numbers. Holder
Master Pictures Corp."*

Discovered: *At rise, the* Casting Director *is at
the 'phone.*

Casting Director. No, no—nothing today. I
know, but I can't write a part in for you. *(As she
hangs up the 'phone)* They're doing the Nile scene

in "The Tiger Woman." Yeh—desert stuff. Won't be back for a week.

(PA MONTAGUE *enters at left. A man slightly over middle age, somewhat seedy, but possessed of a good deal of dignity.*)

MONTAGUE. Good morning. (*Feels for "bar rail" with foot.*) Is it within the possibilities that you could furnish employment for an actor?

CASTING DIRECTOR. Sorry, Mr. Montague. Nothing today.

MONTAGUE. You understand that I am not applying for extra work.

CASTING DIRECTOR. Well, I'll tell you, Mr. Montague—things are pretty dull just now.

MONTAGUE. However, I might be willing to masquerade as an extra for the time being.

(SIGMUND ROSENBLATT, *a director, enters at right with script to film. A Semitic-appearing young man, rather crude.*)

ROSENBLATT. (*Pausing in the doorway to call back to an unseen figure*) All right, Ralph! Don't keep me waitin'!

VOICE. (*Heard off*) Right away!

MONTAGUE. (*Advancing somewhat timidly*) Mr. Rosenblatt——

ROSENBLATT. (*To* CAMERA MAN, *not noticing* MONTAGUE) That's where we lose the time. And they blame we directors.

CAMERA MAN. (*Enters* R.1) Yes, sir.

MONTAGUE. If I might—make so bold——

ROSENBLATT. Got to be a retake on them Chinatown scenes—the fan-tan game.

CAMERA MAN. Yes, sir.

MONTAGUE. Mr. Rosenblatt——

ROSENBLATT. You take all that China stuff—— (*He notices* MONTAGUE.) What is it?

MONTAGUE. If by any chance the scenario calls for a real actor——

ROSENBLATT. All full up. (*Crosses* L. *to* CASTING DIRECTOR.)

MONTAGUE. You may recall that I played a desperado when you were taking——

ROSENBLATT. Oh, yes—what's the name?

MONTAGUE. Montague. Lester Montague.

ROSENBLATT. Haven't got a thing. (*Crosses* L.C. CAMERA MAN *exits* R.)

MONTAGUE. I was with you in "The Little Shepherd of the Bar Z." That was the working title. I believe it was released as "I Want More Children."

ROSENBLATT. Well, water stuff next week. Can you swim?

(WELLER *enters* L.)

MONTAGUE. (*Proudly*) Of course, I am an actor.

ROSENBLATT. Well! (*Calls*) Ralph! Ralph! God, he's a snail!

WELLER. (*A pause*) Say, Commander, I got an idea you and Baxter'll go nuts about.

ROSENBLATT. Well?

WELLER. The place to leave Baxter for the next episode!

ROSENBLATT. What's that?

WELLER. Dangling from the end of the human ladder, two hundred feet up!

ROSENBLATT. (*Judicially*) H'm! Well—maybe.

WELLER. Surest thing you know! And the Chinks shooting at her from the roof!

ROSENBLATT. Not so bad—not so bad! (*As* CAMERA MAN *enters at right.*)

CAMERA MAN. All ready, Chief?

ROSENBLATT.   Come on, now—make it snappy!
We just got a big idea for the end of this instalment!   Came to me like that!

(*'PHONE Ready.*)

(MERTON *enters.   It is* MERTON'S *first visit to this
room, although he has spent several weeks waiting outside the lot.   Naturally he is all eyes.*)

ROSENBLATT.   Listen!   The human ladder swings
Hortense clear from the window ledge when the fire
starts, see—just as we had it.
CAMERA MAN.   I got ye!

(MERTON *is gaping at them, and is about to be
walked into at any second.*)

ROSENBLATT.   Now!   Instead of the reporter res-
cuing her in this instalment—see?—we leave her
hanging there, four hundred feet up!
WELLER.   Aw, say, Chief—that's my idea.

(ROSENBLATT *crosses left.*)

ROSENBLATT.   Just at the finish another Chink
shoots the poisoned bullet from the roof.   (*Still talking, he goes out at left with his camera man.*)

(WELLER *follows out* L., *dazed and scratching his
head.   MERTON, rather dazed, stands looking
after them.   MONTAGUE, left alone center, also
looks after them, but with more resignation in
his glance.   Slowly MERTON shifts his gaze to
the rest of the room, then to MONTAGUE.*)

(*'PHONE.*)

MONTAGUE.   (*Tragically, partly to* MERTON *and*

partly to the whole room) Swim! *(He takes a seat on the bench.)*

(MERTON, *nerving himself for the ordeal, advances to the little window and presents himself. It is the closest that he has yet come to the inside of the game, and his attitude reflects his eager excitement.)*

MERTON. Is—is this where the actors are—selected?

CASTING DIRECTOR. What's that?

MERTON. I say, do you—— That is, are the actors—— Is there likely to be——

CASTING DIRECTOR. *(Comprehending)* Oh! *(Back to the romantic tone again)* Nothing today. Sorry.

(WELLER *enters from* L.)

WELLER. If that scene don't make them howl and fall off their seats! *(Stops near* CASTING DIRECTOR—R. *of her.)* Oh, yes! Say, Countess——

CASTING DIRECTOR. Yes, Mr. Weller?

WELLER. Jeff says he wants a big, bow-legged man for the pig to slip through in that new one.

CASTING DIRECTOR. How big is the pig?

WELLER. Oh, it's a hog.

CASTING DIRECTOR. All right. I know just the fellow!

WELLER. All right. *(He exits* R.)

MERTON. Who does he want the hog for?

CASTING DIRECTOR. For Bert Chester, the cross-eyed man.

MERTON. *(Crosses* R.) He must be acting in a pig pen.

('PHONE.)

CASTING DIRECTOR. *('Phone)* All right, tin

plunky. *(She turns away and* MERTON *has to do likewise. He reads the sign over to himself, then gets up courage to brave the window again.)*

MERTON. *(After waiting a few seconds for the woman to appear)* I—I don't suppose it would be possible—for anybody to—to go inside—would it? I mean just—look around.

CASTING DIRECTOR. *(Giving him a quick look)* Working here?

MERTON. Not yet.

CASTING DIRECTOR. Sorry.

(READY 'Phone.)

*(*MERTON *turns away again, and seems about to depart. But he goes back to the window a third time.)*

MERTON. *(Trying to attract her attention)* Excuse me——

CASTING DIRECTOR. My Lord, you again!

MERTON. I just wanted to ask you——

CASTING DIRECTOR. *(Not unkindly)* There's nothing doing, and you can't go in.

MERTON. I know, but—if there were—something doing—you'd know about it first, wouldn't you?

CASTING DIRECTOR. Yes. Next to Will Hays.

MERTON. Well, then, you wouldn't mind if I waited here a while, would you, just in case—there was something?

CASTING DIRECTOR. Help yourself, but there's only two companies shooting on the lot. *(Speaks into 'phone)* What? Yes, there's one—I sent her in. Oh! *(Hangs up. As she does so* GIRL *enters* L., *sits bench* L.C.)

GIRL. Sixth and last lap! Hello, Pa!

MONTAGUE. *(*R.C.*)* How are you, my dear?

GIRL. All jake, but it's certainly tough on us Extras. I've been in every studio in Hollywood in the last hour and a half. Covered 'em so fast they thought I was a tourist!

MONTAGUE. Conditions *are* discouraging.

GIRL. *(Powders nose)* Tell me they're going to shoot some Arab stuff up at the Consolidated tomorrow, but I says, no thanks—I've been bit by my last camel.

MONTAGUE. *(Wavering still—crosses* L.) Still, any employment would be grateful in times like these.

GIRL. *(Sighs)* Well, you can go to it if you want to. Besides, I'm getting too beautiful for the films. Baxter's jealous of me already.

MONTAGUE. *(On his feet)* You said the Consolidated, I believe?

GIRL. *(Observing* MERTON, *and answering with divided attention)* Huh? Oh—the desert stuff? Yah, but look out for those camels. They sink a pretty tooth.

MONTAGUE. *(About to go)* Oh, I know a remedy for camel bites. *(He goes out at left.)*

GIRL. *(Rises—crosses to* MERTON—*one eye on* MERTON) Hello, Newcomer! *(This to* MERTON.)

MERTON. *(Caught by her mention of Baxter, but feeling a vague animosity toward the Montague girl)* Oh—excuse me, but——

GIRL. Sure.

MERTON. Did you—you didn't mean Beulah Baxter, did you, that was jealous, I mean?

GIRL. Jealous? Last time I starred with her she said she'd quit cold if I kept on arriving in a different automobile every day. Had to *sell* my third assistant Pierce Arrow.

MERTON. But nobody every stars with Beulah Baxter . . .

(READY 'Phone.)

GIRL. Well, I wasn't really starred. My parents wouldn't let me.

MERTON. They wouldn't?

GIRL. Nope. Too young.

MERTON. Ah! *(Walks* R.)

GIRL. *New* on the lot, ain't you?

MERTON. No, not exactly.

GIRL. Didn't remember seeing you before. Still, they come and go.

('PHONE.)

MERTON. *(Quick to agree)* Yes.

CASTING DIRECTOR. *(Calling to the* GIRL) Hello, Flips. *(Into 'phone)* No, nothing today. *(Hangs up.)*

GIRL. Hello, Countess! *(To* MERTON) Excuse me—my public's calling. *(At the window)* Can't you give the camera a little peek at me or at Pa? No, nothing today, dearie! *(Imitating her voice.)*

CASTING DIRECTOR. Pretty dull here. How is it around?

GIRL. Could have gone on in a harem tank scene at the Bigart, but they wanted me to dress like a fish.

CASTING DIRECTOR. You're not so good at that.

GIRL. No. Built more like home folks. But, honest, Countess, can't you give my old dad a little job? He's been stickin' home and lately making old Kentucky bourbon in thirty minutes. If he don't quit he's going to see some moving pictures that nobody else can.

CASTING DIRECTOR. Sorry, but there's nothing—

GIRL. Oh, well . . . *(Turns* R., *then* L.) Say, you haven't seen Jeff Baird around?

CASTING DIRECTOR. He's on the lot some place.

GIRL. I got a date to give him some ideas. Bet he's sitting around not doing a thing—just waiting for me. *(She is starting right, but stops as she observes the highly disgusted* MERTON.) What's the matter, Trouper?

MERTON. Do you—do you have anything to do

with those Jeff Baird things? Those—those comedies?

GIRL. Do I? Countess, tell him who I am!
(Hastily) No, don't—let him find out for himself.
(ROSENBLATT *enters at* L.) Well, if he's on the lot—
(Crosses MERTON *to gate.* MERTON *sits up* C. GIRL
is starting right, but stops as she observes ROSEN-
BLATT.)

CASTING DIRECTOR. Want something, Mr. Rosenblatt?

ROSENBLATT. *(Personifying the very important
man—pays no attention to the* GIRL, *but crosses
quickly to the window—*MERTON *scrambles out of
the way)* Mr. Parmalee been in? *(At the mention
of* PARMALEE, MERTON *becomes very conscious, and
tries his best to look like him.)*

CASTING DIRECTOR. I don't believe so, Mr. Rosenblatt.

ROSENBLATT. Telephone No. 21, and get one of
my assistants. *(Snaps fingers)* I forget his name.
Have him tell Parmalee that the commander is waiting. And hurry—my time's valuable.

CASTING DIRECTOR. Yes, sir. *(Exits into room.
The* GIRL *with a good deal of amusement in her
eyes.)*

GIRL. Oh, Commander!

ROSENBLATT. Yes . . . yes?

GIRL. Could you—could you give me just a minute, please?

ROSENBLATT. Well, I'm very busy, very busy,
but——

GIRL. Well, you see, it's this way, Commander.
I got a great idea for a story, see, and I was thinking who to take it to, and I thought of a lot of them,
and I asked my friends, and they all said, "Oh, take
it to Mr. Rosenblatt, because he's the one director
on the lot that can get every ounce of value out of
it." So I thought—but of course if you're too busy—

ROSENBLATT. I *am* busy, but then, I'm always busy. They run me to death here. Still, it was very *kind* of your friends, and of course . . .

GIRL. Thank you a thousand times, Mr. Rosenblatt. *(She assumes a worshipping pose.)* It starts off kind of like this. You see, I'm a Hawaiian princess. Oh, excuse me. Well, anyway, I'm this Hawaiian princess and my father, Old King Mauna Loa, dies and leaves me two thousand volcanoes and a billiard cue. Now——

ROSENBLATT. Ah—just a minute. A billiard cue?

(CASTING DIRECTOR enters.)

GIRL. Yes, sir. *(Nods.)* And every morning I have to go out and ram it down the volcanoes to see if they're all right. Now, then——

ROSENBLATT. What are you *talking* about?

(MERTON comes down right of GIRL.)

GIRL. The *villain* is very wealthy, and owns one of the largest ukulele plantations on the island . . .

ROSENBLATT. Tush, tush! Absurd, absurd! *(He walks toward CASTING DIRECTOR.)* Any word yet?

GIRL. Oh, dear! Well, of course, I knew it was crude—but no one ever listens to you until you break into the magazines. Really, really, said Miss Montague—termed by many the most beautiful woman in the world . . . *(Crosses to MERTON to gate R.)* I am at a loss to understand why the public should be so interested in me. What can I say to your readers? Oh, please, please go away and leave me to my books and my art! *(She exits right.)*

ROSENBLATT. *(At C.D)* Yes, yes, all right—all right . . . *(ROSENBLATT starts right, and, as he does so, meets with MERTON.)*

MERTON. *(As ROSENBLATT, observing him, stops*

pacing) I—I knew in a minute her scenario wasn't any good—myself.

ROSENBLATT. *(Regarding him)* How's that?

MERTON. *(Fussed)* Yes, sir.

ROSENBLATT. What?

MERTON. I say, the minute she said all those volcanoes.

ROSENBLATT. What, what, what!

MERTON. Why, I knew right away it wouldn't—that is—it wouldn't be practical——

(WELLER *enters at right.*)

WELLER. He's on the way—I just talked to one of his valets. (ROSENBLATT *grunts.*)

CASTING DIRECTOR. Here you are, Mr. Rosenblatt.

ROSENBLATT. *(To her)* Oh, yes—yes——

MERTON. *(Awed, has worked close to* WELLER) Is—is Harold Parmalee coming here?

WELLER. *(Regarding him)* Where'd *you* come from?

MERTON. *(Nervously)* Sir?

WELLER. Not that it matters. *(Crosses* L. *to* ROSENBLATT.)

ROSENBLATT. *(Stops pacing)* You know, if this stuff looks all right today, we can get back on Crusoe in the morning.

WELLER. That's fine.

ROSENBLATT. I'm anxious to get that under way.

WELLER. Great idea of yours—Robinson Crusoe.

ROSENBLATT. And it'll be a great picture, the way I treat it. Can't you imagine—— *(Starts* R., *sees* MERTON.) Good heavens, who is that boy, anyhow? Go away—go away—sit down some place! (MERTON *backs off* C., *sits.*) Now where was I?

WELLER. Robinson Crusoe.

ROSENBLATT. Oh, yes. Well, I've got it all doped out. What happens is this.

(HAROLD PARMALEE, *a film star who looks the part, enters at right.* MERTON *is so excited at his appearance that he can hardly move, comes down.*)

PARMALEE. Good morning.

WELLER. Good morning, Mr. Parmalee.

ROSENBLATT. Oh, hello, Harold. I was just telling Weller about the Crusoe stuff. (MERTON *goes* L. *of* PARMALEE.) The way we work it is this. Friday—Friday has a sister, see—only she can't be his real sister because she's white—— Get what I mean?

PARMALEE. Yes, I noticed that.

ROSENBLATT. Well, we'll work it out later. She's the daughter of an English Earl that was wrecked near the Island, and Friday's mother brought her up as her own child. She's saved the papers that came ashore and she has the Earl's coat-of-arms tatooed on her shoulder blade. Get this finish, Weller—and finally, after Robinson Crusoe has fallen in love with her, along comes the old Earl, her father, in a ship that rescues them all. What do you think? Great, isn't it?

WELLER. Great!

ROSENBLATT. Now come on and let's look at this stuff. In that way we get the sex into it. (ROSENBLATT *and* WELLER *exit* R.)

(PARMALEE *is about to follow when* MERTON *halts him.*)

MERTON. (*Crosses to* PARMALEE, *his heart in his mouth*) Mr. . . . Mr. Parmalee, Mr. Parmalee——

PARMALEE. (R.C., *condescendingly*) Yes, old chap?

MERTON. (C.) I have long been one of your admirers, and appreciate the fine things that you are trying to do in screen art.

(PARMALEE *looks at him, then reaches into pocket and takes out elaborate watch.*)

PARMALEE. *(Good-naturedly)* I suppose you want to see the watch.

MERTON. *(Then eagerly taking it in his hand)* Oh, that's the one they gave you.

PARMALEE. *(Explaining it)* Five thousand exhibitors representing forty-two States. (PARMALEE *takes watch back, smiles, holds it in his hand.*)

MERTON. A wonderful trophy. *(He continues hastily.* PARMALEE *halts again.*) But—what I was going to say was—I want to do something artistic myself. I read—in your last interview—that you always encouraged beginners and——

PARMALEE. *(Trying to escape)* Oh, yes, yes!

MERTON. And I—I'm really coming to what I was going to say now—because I thought maybe you might be especially interested in me because—because—— *(He is trying his best to look like* PARMALEE *at this instant.*) Well, do you notice—anything?

PARMALEE. Do I what?

MERTON. *(Posing himself)* Do you—notice anything?

PARMALEE. *(Sniffing)* I don't think so.

MERTON. No—no—I mean—now, you see, you're standing that way, and I'm standing just the same way—see? I mean, in the way *you* look and the way *I* look—do you notice anything?

PARMALEE. Really, I don't know what you're talking about.

MERTON. Well, I mean—don't you think we— that is, that I look——

PARMALEE. What? This is all very silly . . . very silly indeed! *(Exits right.)*

(CASTING DIRECTOR *enters.* MERTON—*a pretty crushed* MERTON—*is left alone as he watches* PARMALEE *depart. Then, in a calmer mood, he walks over to the bench, sits—then to* CASTING DIRECTOR.)

MERTON. *(Peering within)* Say!
CASTING DIRECTOR. *(Suddenly appearing, and observing that it is* MERTON *again)* For God's sake!
MERTON. Well, I thought——
CASTING DIRECTOR. (MERTON *walks over and sits on the bench)* There's nothing doing and you can't go in!

(MERTON *then remembers exit of* PARMALEE, *goes to gate, and putting on his hat, poses himself the way he saw* PARMALEE.)

MERTON. It's all very silly, very silly indeed!
CASTING DIRECTOR. *(Who has been watching him)* Well!
MERTON. *(Turns quickly and takes off hat, grins sheepishly)* Ma'am?
CASTING DIRECTOR. I suppose your trunks are coming?
MERTON. I suppose you mean my—costumes?
CASTING DIRECTOR. You're new, aren't you?
MERTON. *(Reluctantly)* Well, I am now, but I won't be!
CASTING DIRECTOR. Have you registered?
MERTON. Ma'am?
CASTING DIRECTOR. Have I got your name and address?
MERTON. Oh—no. *(Crosses L.)*
CASTING DIRECTOR. You *are* new. *(She has picked up a pencil.)* Come on.
MERTON. Ma'am?

CASTING DIRECTOR. What's your name? You've got a name, haven't you?

MERTON. *(Whispers name, important)* Clifford Armytage.

CASTING DIRECTOR. *(The pencil poised)* Come again.

MERTON. Clifford Armytage.

CASTING DIRECTOR. Clifford Armytage? Well, why not? *(She writes.)* Address?

MERTON. Two thousand four hundred and sixty, Oakdale Avenue.

CASTING DIRECTOR. Line of parts?

MERTON. Huh?

CASTING DIRECTOR. What's your line?

MERTON. Oh! Well, that's what I was going to show you. *(He draws out the art photographs and gives them to her.)* You see, those'll give you a pretty good idea. I mean, that's——

CASTING DIRECTOR. *(Inspecting)* Oh, my goodness! You don't mean these are all the same person?

MERTON. *(Proudly)* They are, though.

CASTING DIRECTOR. Oh, what do you think of that? Cowboy, and—society man, and—now don't tell me that's you with the horse!

MERTON. *(Taking them back)* Yes—well, of course. I just wanted you to see what I could do. Of course, I wouldn't expect big parts to begin with. I'm willing to work hard and sacrifice in the beginning.   *('PHONE Ready.)*

CASTING DIRECTOR. *(Looking at photographs)* You'll sacrifice, all right. *(Photos in book.)*

MERTON. Because it's only out of hard work and sacrifice that the finer things come, and you take Beulah Baxter or Harold Parmalee, or any of them, and they all started that way.

CASTING DIRECTOR. *(Regarding him)* Say, you're a regular bug, aren't you?

MERTON. *(Looking around)* Say—say—does Beulah Baxter—does she ever come in this way?

CASTING DIRECTOR. Sure—mostly.

MERTON. Right along here?

CASTING DIRECTOR. Just like a mortal.

MERTON. *(Turns and surveys the room, worshippingly, then turns back to the window)* Is—is Beulah Baxter married?

CASTING DIRECTOR. Let me see. I never can remember.

MERTON. She's the little wonder woman, all right. I'll bet you she sacrificed before she got up to where she is.

('PHONE.)

CASTING DIRECTOR. *I'll* say she did! *(Hold for laugh. In 'phone)* Yes, yes, I understand—stage eight, all right.

MERTON. I don't suppose you could fix it so that I could work in a picture with her—some time?

CASTING DIRECTOR. Now listen, son. I might not be able to get you *anything* for a long, long time.

MERTON. Oh, I don't mind—struggling. The only thing is—I want to do something really significant, and not just—comedies.

CASTING DIRECTOR. Well, I'll remember you. And I can always reach you at two thousand four hundred and so forth?

MERTON. Yes, only—during the day I'll be right here.

CASTING DIRECTOR. *(Gives him a look)* All day?

MERTON. Yeh!

CASTING DIRECTOR. Aren't you ever going to try the other studios?

MERTON. Oh, no!

CASTING DIRECTOR. Well, I ought to enjoy that.

(The MONTAGUE GIRL *enters right, accompanied by* JEFF BAIRD, *the Buckeye Comedy King. He is*

rather a bluff soul with a prominent mustache.
GIRL *talking gaily as she enters.* MERTON, *his
distaste evident, is already backing away.)*

GIRL. That's the stuff, Jeff! Then when he tries
to get up, the chandelier drops right on him. But
the gag is, instead of breaking, it's a rubber chandelier and it bounces—see?

BAIRD. Great! I'll get you a little check for
that.

GIRL. It's all right, Jeff—I like you and that
makes it all jake with me. *(To* MERTON*)* Hello,
Trouper! Still hanging on?

MERTON. *(Forced to reply)* I—guess so.

GIRL. Well, you stick to it—that's the way I get
my success. Jeff, meet my friend, the *trouper*.
(Crosses L.*)* Trouper, Mr. Jeff Baird, the *Buckeye
Comedy King.*

BAIRD. *(Putting out his hand)* How are you,
kid? What's your line—comedy?

MERTON. *(Shaking hands with great dignity)*
No, sir. It is my wish to do something of a finer
nature than mere comedies. *(GIRL—her hand going suddenly to her head, in mock terror.* CASTING
DIRECTOR *exits.)* And I would not even entertain
an offer to associate myself with them. *(He turns
and walks away right.)*

BAIRD. *(Crosses to* GIRL—*after a moment)* Is
that final?

GIRL. So help me God!

BAIRD. *(Looks after* MERTON*)* It certainly
messes up *my* plans. *(Laughs.)* Come on—— *(He
crosses her to* L.I.*)* Let's go over and see those
rushes.

GIRL. *(Absorbed in thought of* MERTON*)* You
get 'em ready. I'll come right over!

BAIRD. *(With an understanding look from the*

girl to MERTON) Want to take soundings, eh?

GIRL. Uh, huh!

BAIRD. All right—I'll look for you in ten minutes. *(He goes out left.)*

(MERTON *is wrapped in disdainful dignity. She pauses squarely in front of him.)*

GIRL. *(Crosses* R. *to* MERTON) Hello, Kid!

MERTON. *(Compelled to reply, but keeping his dignity)* Good morning.

GIRL. How about a little dialogue? Name your own weapons.

MERTON. I—haven't anything to say.

GIRL. Sure you have—you're just modest. Come on over here and talk it over. (MERTON *goes unwillingly. He and the* GIRL *come down stage.)* That's the stuff—be sociable. Now tell me, what have you got against poor Jeff Baird?

MERTON. *(Compelled to defend himself)* I don't like his comedies. They degrade a—an art.

GIRL. Well, now we're getting some place. *(She turns to him suddenly and whispers)* What art?

MERTON. *(With dignity)* The art of the motion picture.

GIRL. *(Changing her key)* You haven't been around here long. (MERTON *is silent.)* Huh?

MERTON. I—I don't care to discuss my—private affairs. *(Crosses* R., *turns back.)*

GIRL. All right, kid. Only take an old trouper's word for it—it's a tough game. Work is few and far between, and when it does come, it's generally pretty cheesy. You take even an old-timer like Pa. Last month he got a job in a moonshining play.

MERTON. You mean where the revenue officer falls in love with the moonshiner's daughter?

GIRL. That's it. Well, anyhow, Pa gets this job and they won't stand for the crepe hair, so he has to go and raise a garden. *Gives a month to raising it* —all his spare time—and what happens?

MERTON. I'm sure I don't know.

GIRL. *After four days' work* they go and have him killed off. Pa goes around for a week and tries to rent the garden, but by that time nobody was doing anything but Chinese pictures. That's what you're up against in *this* game, kid.

MERTON. But I couldn't raise a beard anyhow.

GIRL. *(A pause)* You win. (MERTON *starts to turn away. Crosses L. She follows.)* Say!

MERTON. Well?

GIRL. You understand I'm not inquisitive or anything, but—don't you think I've been doing a lot of talking?

MERTON. Oh, I don't know.

GIRL. How long you been around here?

MERTON. About—three weeks.

GIRL. Funny I didn't see you before.

MERTON. I wasn't—I didn't know about this place.

GIRLL. Where were you?

MERTON. Out there.

GIRL. On the street? For three weeks?

MERTON. *(Melting a little)* Oh, I didn't mind it.

GIRL. You're hell on being an actor, ain't you?

MERTON. I expected I'd have to struggle.

GIRL. Well, don't say I didn't warn you.

MERTON. Thanks. *(He is about to turn away left.)*

GIRL. Hold on—don't go. *(She sits.)* That's right. Come on over here and sit down. *(He does so. He halts.)* Where'd you come from—before you come here?

MERTON. I—came from a little town. *(Sits L. of her.)*

GIRL. Still afraid of me, ain't you?

MERTON. Oh, no, I'm not.

GIRL. Well, don't you be. I'm just a poor mug, the same as you, only I've been at it a little longer, that's all. I like you.

MERTON. *(Very fussed)* Well, it isn't—I don't want you to think I don't appreciate——

GIRL. That's all right. You're a nice kid, only you're awful green. Don't think I talk to all of them like this, but somehow there's something about you that made me do it; if you want somebody to pilot you around, maybe introduce you at the other studios——

MERTON. Oh, no—thanks. I—I'm going to work just at this studio, if you don't mind.

GIRL. What's the big notion?

MERTON. Well, you see—what I want—— *(Laughs—crosses to c. He is quite fussed.)* I mean, this is the company where Beulah Baxter is, and I figured——

GIRL. *(Rises—regarding him closely)* Say, kid, look at me. *(He does so.)* You haven't gone and fallen in love with a picture, have you?

MERTON. *(Gulping)* I—I didn't say that.

GIRL. I know you didn't, but I'm awful quick.

MERTON. It is merely that I am a great admirer of Miss Baxter's art, and regard her as the wonder woman of the silver screen.

GIRL. Honest?

(READY 'Phone.)

MERTON. You—of course you were only joking about starring with her, weren't you? Because she doesn't ever have anybody. She doesn't even have anybody ever double for her, the way some of them do when it's dangerous.

GIRL. Oh!

MERTON. So I thought if I could only get with her company, I mean no matter how small a part it was, why, I thought I'd rather do that than go to one of the other studios and maybe work with some-body who—whose ideals weren't as fine as hers.

GIRL. I see.

MERTON. You—you don't know of anybody whose ideals are as fine as hers—do you?

GIRL. No. She's got the finest set of ideals on the lot. *(The 'phone rings.* CASTING DIRECTOR *answers—her voice is unheard in the beginning.)* She's certainly the—— What was it you called her?

MERTON. The wonder woman of the silver screen.

GIRL. That was it.

MERTON. That was the appellation *Photoland* gave her when——

CASTING DIRECTOR. *(Into 'phone)* All right, Mr. Rosenblatt. Nine of them!

GIRL. My God, it's work! *(She grabs* MERTON *by the arm and pulls him toward the window.)*

CASTING DIRECTOR. Evening clothes. Stage No. Six at eight-thirty in the morning. Society stuff with Harold Parmalee in Robinson Crusoe. Don't for-get—evening things, jewelry, and all you've got! Wear your best, Flips.

MERTON. *(Bobbing around)* Will you please let me——

CASTING DIRECTOR. Eight-thirty tomorrow morn-ing on Stage No. Six. Here's your ticket—full eve-ning dress! Have you got evening dress?

MERTON. *(Excited)* Yes!

CASTING DIRECTOR. Atta baby! *(Pats shoulder.)*

MERTON. And I want to thank you——

CASTING DIRECTOR. Harold Parmalee in "Robin-son Crusoe."

(PA MONTAGUE rushes on at left, making straight for the window.)

MONTAGUE. I understand—that is, I was just informed——

CASTING DIRECTOR. All right, Mr. Montague. Here's your ticket.

MONTAGUE. There will be *one* actor in this picture! When I was with Barrett——

CASTING DIRECTOR. Eight-thirty tomorrow morning—Stage No. Six.

MONTAGUE. *(As he turns away)* Oh, yes. *(He sees his daughter.)* And I almost lost this opportunity for your camels.

GIRL. What's the matter—were they full up?

MONTAGUE. They were not. It wasn't camels. It was wild-cats. *(Exits left.)*

GIRL. H'm. Well, kid, you're going to be an actor now, all right. You know, Countess, there's only one thing gets me.

CASTING DIRECTOR. What's that?

GIRL. Who the devil wears evening clothes in "Robinson Crusoe"?

MERTON. *(To CASTING DIRECTOR)* Say, should—should I have my breakfast before I come in the morning?

CASTING DIRECTOR. It might not be a bad idea.

MERTON. *(To the MONTAGUE GIRL)* We're to have breakfast first, before we get here.

GIRL. Those who *can* eat.

MERTON. *(Stands in sheer excitement for a moment, his eyes sparkling—finally looks at his watch)* It's about two o'clock now. That's—not so long, is it?

GIRL. No time at all.

MERTON. I mean, if I go to bed early, why, that'll make the time pass so much more quickly.

GIRL. *(To the CASTING DIRECTOR)* I didn't think it was possible.

MERTON. What?

GIRL. Nothing.

MERTON. *(His face alight with a new idea—rushes to the window)* I—I'm working here now!

CASTING DIRECTOR. So?

MERTON. You remember before I asked if I could go in, and you asked if I was working here? Well, now I am! *(He waits in suspense for the decision.)*

(The CASTING DIRECTOR *looks up at the* MONTAGUE GIRL, *who nods.)*

CASTING DIRECTOR. Why, sure. Help yourself. *(Hands him card.)*

MERTON. *(In a trance, and unaware that the* GIRL *is the one to be thanked)* Thanks. *(He starts to walk toward the door at right—there is a noise off* L.)

VOICE. *(Off* L.) Make way, there!

MERTON. *(To the* GIRL) Who is it?

GIRL. I think it's a friend of yours.

MERTON. Not—you mean—Beulah Baxter?

(Then BAXTER *enters* L., *crosses and exits* R. *Then* MERTON, *who has watched every move, slowly follows. As he starts—)*

CURTAIN

ACT III

Scene I

Scene: *The scene is Stage No. Six on the Holden lot. A typical motion picture studio stage, inclosed in glass. Left of center a rich interior has been set up. There are only two walls, set at such an angle that the audience may clearly see what is going on inside them, and also so that those on the clear part of the stage may have an unobstructed view. This scene, occupying about half the stage, presents a luxurious room. There are tapestries, paintings, rugs and fine furniture. There is a library table about in the center of this room; there is a desk prominently placed; there are chairs to fill. As for the stage as a whole, it is not inclosed at the sides. Entrances are made at right and left. There are two motion picture cameras, somewhere down R. A chair with its back to the audience. Across its back, in neat letters, is printed:* MR. ROSENBLATT. MERTON *sits on it, hidden by an extra. The time is about two-thirty o'clock on the following day. Stage is lighted by "hard" lights, "floor" and "overhead" banks.*

WELLER *is present, of course; there is a man at camera, others at the lights.* PARMALEE, *in evening clothes, is on the set;* MURIEL, *in evening clothes, is seated center;* ROSENBLATT, *megaphone in hand, is at her right, directing her. Cameras in action.* MAX, *the violinist, is playing as curtain rises.*

ROSENBLATT. That's it! That's it! Hold it! Getting it, Phil? That's the stuff! Your heart's

breaking, you're absolutely miserable. Give me tears
—give me tears! Everything is terrible—things
couldn't be worse! There's been a big earthquake,
the ship's gone down! Don't cover your face with
your handkerchief—we're taking your face, not the
hair on your head!—I'm getting worse!—You can't
have that car! More tears! Damn it!—more tears!
Oh, my God, but you're miserable!—All right—save
it!

WELLER. Save it! *(Whistle. Lights go off.)*

ROSENBLATT. *(Crosses L.)* That's the flash back,
Harold—when you sit there thinking. We'll take
some more of it tomorrow. Shift, Weller!

WELLER. Shift? *(Whistle.)*

ROSENBLATT. No, Muriel!

MURIEL. Yeh?

ROSENBLATT. We'll take some more of that tomorrow. So be here promptly.

MURIEL. All right, sweetheart. *(She exits L.U.E.)*

ROSENBLATT. Not here, not here! Now, Harold,
ready for you! (HAROLD *down* L. *of* ROSENBLATT.)
We're back in your rooms.—Now everybody get this.
You, Harold, are—— *(After an interval)*—Schuy-
ler Van Rennselaer, a New York society man. We'll
use those shots of you on a polo pony, Harold—but
he's sick of the whole game. Now for this new
scene! In the midst of a party, when he has a whole
lot of guests—he goes to—— *(Sits on* MERTON'S
lap—gets up and bows to MERTON.) I beg your
pardon!

MERTON. *(Scrambling out of the way)* Ex—excuse me! *(He crosses L.)*

ROSENBLATT. Good Lord! Now where was I?
(GIRL *on.)* Where was I? Where was I?

WELLER. He has a whole lot of guests.

ROSENBLATT. Yes—he has a whole lot of guests.
(Turn to MERTON.) Idiot! *(To* HAROLD) Society people. And he turns on them and bawls them

out—— There's a big kick for you, Harold—and says he's going to go some place and live alone. The simple life—see? And somebody says, "Oh, like Robinson Crusoe?" Only we introduce it natural with the book on the table. *(Takes book from table.)* And he says, "Yes—that's just what he's going to do—live on an island like Robinson Crusoe." Then he drives them all out, and settles down in a chair to think. He takes up the book, begins to look through it, and here's the big kick. *(Rap on table.)* He *dreams* he's Robinson Crusoe. *(Book down.* WELLER *indulges in a long, low whistle, implying that the majesty of the idea is too much for words to express.* ROSENBLATT *turns to him.)* Like it?

WELLER. Big stuff, Chief.

PARMALEE. Ah—how about the scene—ah—you know, the scene in the book about—fifteen men on a dead man's chest? Do you show that later?

ROSENBLATT. *(Puzzled)* I don't just remember that. As a matter of fact, I just skimmed that passage.

PARMALEE. Well, I thought that would be rather a good scene, you know. The—the dead man, and all that.

ROSENBLATT. Yes, I thought that was in Monte Cristo. *(*GIRL *talking to* MERTON *l.c.)*

WELLER. I don't think that is in Crusoe.

PARMALEE. Well, I remember as a child . . .

GIRL. Excuse me, Mr. Rosenblatt.

ROSENBLATT. Yes—what is it?

GIRL. I think that's from Romeo and Juliet. *(*GIRL *to* MERTON.)*

ROSENBLATT. Oh, yes, the court-room scene—— *(Cross* R.*)* Well, now we'll start presently. I've got to think it over—I want to get just the right atmosphere. How'll we begin? *(Cross* L.*)*

WELLER. Can I help you, **Commander?**

Rosenblatt. *(Pace)* No, no, I must work these things out myself. Now, let's see—which is the best method to reach the big moment—— *(Sits center, thinking.)*

Weller. *(Calling off* R.*)* Max—oh! Max—here with your fiddle——

(Max *enters right with fiddle.*)

Rosenblatt. Haven't you a harp?

Weller. Got a harp?

Max. No, sir——

Rosenblatt. H'm—well, go ahead—— Oh! *(As* Max *begins to play very loudly,* Rosenblatt *tries to shut out the sound.)* No, no, no! Give me a Venetian motive!

(Max *resumes playing.* Rosenblatt *paces;* Max *walks after him, playing. They pace up and down, followed by* Merton, *intent on seeing how it is done.* Rosenblatt, Violinist *and* Merton *exit* R.*)*

Girl. Oh, Weller, the guy they need for this picture is Fritz Kreisler.

(Rosenblatt *enters, followed by the* Violinist, *who is still playing, and then they cross* R. Girl R.C.)

Rosenblatt. *(Clapping his hands)* Come, come!

(Cameraman. *Ring bell.)*

Weller. Come, now—Mr. Rosenblatt's ready. Did you get it, Chief?

(Rosenblatt *enters* R. *and comes* L.*)*

ROSENBLATT. *(Nods)* I'm just in the mood. Now, then, Harold, this retake—prominent young clubman, lavish home—lots of class—and just a little bit bored. *You* remember?

PARMALEE. Oh, by the way. *(Produces a rich dressing-gown.)* Suppose I have this on, and then take it off and put on my dinner coat. It's rather a good bit. They *do* it.

ROSENBLATT. All right, all right! You remember: you're thinking, "Oh, if I could get away from it all!" See?

PARMALEE. I can do it!

ROSENBLATT. *(Cross* R.*)* I'm sure you can. Give him some music, there! Society stuff.

WELLER. *(Calling right)* Society music . . .

(MAX *begins to play.*)

ROSENBLATT. Now, then, everybody ready—lights!

WELLER. Kick it! *(Whistle.)*

ROSENBLATT. Ready, Phil?

WELLER. Just a minute, Commander—— *(He walks toward door* L.U.E.*)* This door has to be closed. *(Speaks to spotlight man.)* And you up there—be sure and keep those spots directly on him. *(Talks to* ROSENBLATT.*)* Take a look at the set, Commander—— *(Walks back to his camera.)*

ROSENBLATT. *(Looking through the blue glass)* Just right, Weller!—Now, Harold!—More poise, more poise! How about you, Weller?

WELLER. All right, Commander.

ROSENBLATT. Camera—that's it—take your time —you're thinking, "Oh, if I could get away from it all!"——

PARMALEE. All right—— *(Sit.)*

ROSENBLATT. Camera! *(Camera begins to grind.)* That's the stuff—you're dead tired—you've been dancing till six o'clock—you're sick of the whole

game—nothing means a thing to you—you're all in—
you're tired—save it!

WELLER. Save it!

*(The lights go off with a clank; the music stops.
    WELLER rushes in front of the camera, holding
    up a numbered slate. PARMALEE relaxes,
    rises.)*

ROSENBLATT. *(Crosses up* R. *to* L., *then* L. *to* R.)
All right—all right! Let's get some of this *house*
stuff.

WELLER. House stuff.

PARMALEE. Ah—the scene with the dressing-
gown.

ROSENBLATT. Oh, all right, all right. Camera—
(Cameras turn and PARMALEE *removes coat and gets
into his dressing-gown.)* Come on, Harold, not too
much footage—it's just a five-reeler—save it.

WELLER. Save it.

ROSENBLATT. Now we'll take the house stuff—

WELLER. House stuff.

ROSENBLATT. You people get around to this side
for the house stuff and make it snappy. Shake a
leg! (WELLER *sends* MERTON *up to* L.C. *Standing
back of center table with book in his hand.)* This
isn't right. Isn't Robinson Crusoe in two volumes?
(WELLER *signals that he doesn't know.)* Oh! All
right. Now I want somebody to come down and discover this book on the table. *(To* MERTON) Think
you can do that?

MERTON. *(Comes down)* I can, sir.

ROSENBLATT. All right—you'll do. You find the
book on the table, see? It's "Robinson Crusoe" and
you're a little surprised. It isn't the book you'd expect to find on a gentleman's table. Then you say:
"Ah!"—let's hear that sub-title, Weller.

WELLER. *(Reading it)* I see you are a book-worm.

ROSENBLATT. *Splendid!* Then, Harold, *you* say —what is it? *(Snap fingers.)*

WELLER. "Yes, that is 'Robinson Crusoe,' a fascinating romance, and one of the greatest stories ever written. There are times when I envy him."

ROSENBLATT. Exactly! Now run through that. There's the book—see? You come down *casually* and discover it—— *(Moves table down.)* I'll just move this table down and get a better perspective. Now run through that. (ROSENBLATT *sits right and* MERTON *goes up, smiling at the* GIRL *as he does so, then he walks down to the table.)* No! No! Not as if you knew you were going to find it—accidental! Try it again! (MERTON *tries it again, but does not do it much better.* ROSENBLATT *turns with disgust.)* All right—you discover the book—pick it up. (MERTON *gives a sharp reaction of surprise upon discovering the book; starts back as though struck.* ROSENBLATT *throws MSS. on floor and paces—*R. *to* L., L. *to* R.*)* No—no—nothing like it—— *(Goes up to* MERTON, *holds book in front of his nose.)* It's a book, not a rattlesnake. *(Slams book down.)* Didn't you ever see a book before?

MERTON. Yes, sir.

ROSENBLATT. I don't believe it—I can't waste—

GIRL. Mr. Rosenblatt——

ROSENBLATT. Yes, yes——?

GIRL. I think if you give him another chance he could do it.

ROSENBLATT. All right—try it again. *(Sits right.* MERTON *falls back, and approaches this time with elaborate carelessness. He finds the book with extreme lanquor.* ROSENBLATT, *head in hands, crosses* L. *to table.)* No—no—that won't do at all! No—no! *(Goes to* MERTON.*)* We've got to get——

Oh, Lord! It certainly takes it out of a man mentally.

MERTON. Well, I think I understand now—if you'll let me try again.

ROSENBLATT. No, no, my nerves are going. I must do something new.

WELLER. You ought to take a rest, Commander.

ROSENBLATT. Oh, I don't mind it when I get something in return, but these extras that they give me—bah!

WELLER. I'd knock off, Commander—you're all in! It's been a long day.

ROSENBLATT. I *am* wearied. My brain——

WELLER. Call 'em again tomorrow.

ROSENBLATT. *(Considering it)* Perhaps you're right. I must feel fresh.

WELLER. Shall I tell them?

ROSENBLATT. I will. *(He raises his voice.)* That's all today. Everybody again at eight-thirty tomorrow morning, same clothes and make up.

WELLER. Eight-thirty tomorrow morning.

(Camera is taken off by CAMERA MAN.*)*

MERTON. Mr. Rosenblatt.

ROSENBLATT. Oh, yes, you—you needn't bother to report tomorrow morning.

MERTON. Sir?

ROSENBLATT. Mr. Weller will give you your pay order.

MERTON. You mean—I wasn't any good?

ROSENBLATT. I—I need a different type for this sort of thing, that's all. *(He calls)* Tim! *(He starts to move off toward* R. VOICE *off* R.*)*

VOICE. Yes, sir?

ROSENBLATT. Just leave this whole set where it is. I'm going to use it again in the morning. *(Down stage* R. *a couple of steps.)*

Voice. *(Off)*   Yes, sir.

Weller.   All right, boys, you're through for the day.

Merton.   But Mr. Rosenblatt——

Rosenblatt. *(Speaking off)* Oh! You're not to touch a thing, understand.

Voice. *(Off)*   Yes, sir.

Merton.   Mr. Rosenblatt, can't I?

Rosenblatt.   And Weller——

Weller.   Yes, sir.

Rosenblatt.   Now I want——

Merton. *(Follows* Rosenblatt *down)*   All I ask is to speak to you just for——

(MUSIC Off r.*)*

Rosenblatt.   What, what is it?   What do you want?

Merton.   If you could only give me one more chance——

Rosenblatt.   Good heavens—I can't use you! Isn't that enough? Coming, Weller? *(Cross* r.*)*

Weller.   Yes—yes. Here's your pay check. *(Hands it to* Merton.*)*

Rosenblatt. *(To violinist)*   Oh, Max!

Max. *(Entering)*   Yes, sir?

Rosenblatt.   I'm going to dope out a new scene in my office.   I want you and your fiddle.

Max.   All right, sir.

Rosenblatt.   Now don't go away.

Max.   No, sir. *(Exits right.)*

Rosenblatt.   Now, Weller, this island stuff that we're going to get—— (Rosenblatt *and* Weller *exit* r.*)*

Girl. *(Left of* Merton*)*   It's—it's all right, kid. That doesn't mean anything.   You'll get lots of bumps like that.

Merton.   No, thanks, I——

Girl. *(Crosses* r.c.*)*   The big bum's crazy, that's all. *(She forces herself back to the optimistic mood.)*

But don't let it do anything to you. They—they can't put you down, can they?

MERTON. I'm not—down. *(Crosses L., over table.)*

GIRL. Of course you're not.

MERTON. I didn't know what he meant—when—

GIRL. Who does?

MERTON. When a person's making their first appearance and all—why——

GIRL. Sure. I know. Why, the first time they aimed a camera at me I thought there was bullets in it.

MERTON. But still, it *was* my chance, and I had to go and—fail.

GIRL. Fail? Just because of a little thing like that? Why, you're going to succeed big. All you need is—confidence in yourself.

MERTON. Is it?

GIRL. That's all most of them have.

MERTON. *(Eager)* But I wish he'd given me another chance. I could have done it the next time. *(Braces up.)*

GIRL. I know! Don't you worry about *him.* Why, he even fired Parmalee once.

MERTON. He did? *(Thinks it over.)* I know I could act the way Parmelee does if I—practiced enough.

GIRL. Of course you could. The only thing is— *(She stops.)*

MERTON. What?

GIRL.. Well—sometimes it takes a long while before you really—that is, before they give you a chance.

MERTON. Oh, I *want* to struggle.

GIRL. *(Quickly)* Yah, but—if it *should* take a while—I mean before you—well—are you fixed all right—for it? Money, I mean?

MERTON. *(Turning away)* Oh—yes.

GIRL. *(Watching him narrowly)* That's good. *Say,* maybe I can get you something over at the Bigart next week.

MERTON. Oh, no, thanks. You remember—-I want to work only at this studio.

GIRL. Still sticking to that idea, eh?

MERTON. Oh, yes. Yes, indeed. Do you think— do you think there'd be any chance of my getting into her company—Miss Baxter's, I mean?

GIRL. Well, I wouldn't work with her just yet, if I were you.

MERTON. You wouldn't? Why not?

GIRL. Oh, I don't know. I just wouldn't. *(Turn R.)*

MERTON. Oh, but I want to. That's one of the things I came out for.

GIRL. Well, if that's what you insist on doing— *(Cross R.)*

MERTON. I bet if I got with her I could learn how to act. And then if I practiced myself at the same time——

GIRL. And you're—you're sure you've got plenty of money?

MERTON. Oh, I don't care about that. I mean, what does money matter when—when—— You just watch me. *(Boasts)* I'll practice, and some time when I'm acting with Miss Baxter, why, Mr. Rosenblatt will come along, and——

GIRL. *(Pause)* Well, there's nobody can say you're not *trying. (Pause.)* Coming?

MERTON. Oh, no. I don't want to go off the lot —just yet. I mean—— *(He looks involuntarily at the table and book.)*

GIRL. Suit yourself. Sure you're not *coming?*

MERTON. Not—just yet.

GIRL. Well—will I find you around—some time?

MERTON. Oh, yes. I'll be on the lot. *(To table.)*

GIRL. That's good. And—so will I—if—the time ever comes when you need me. So-long!

MERTON. So-long! *(She goes.)*

(MUSIC Off R.)

(MERTON, left alone, quickly rearranges the book on the table. He plays the book scene over again, with pathetic eagerness. He walks down stage, as before, picks up the book, then he pauses, and brushes away a tear. Music swells. He keeps at it—goes up again. He comes down perfectly, times all gestures perfectly, picks up book with slow, graceful motion, and a boyish grin of pleasure comes over his face at knowing he has done this correctly.)

CURTAIN

ACT III

Scene II

Scene: *Elsewhere on the lot—a night scene. On stage* R. *a boat—below it are the waves.*

Rosenblatt, *the director, is standing center, directing operations.*

Rosenblatt. *(Before curtain up)* Now, Harry, you understand this is your camera line—catching this point of the boat—you'll get your flashes through the lightning—— *(Curtain up.)* And Harry—try to cut under the bowsprit. All right, boys. Now stand ready on those lights and don't let them wobble —I don't want a retake on this and I don't want to stay here all night. Now watch them—— *(Start* L.*)*

(Beulah *enters* L.)

Beulah. How's this?

Rosenblatt. All right—— *(Exits* L. Weller *enters* L.*)*

Weller. You forgot your cape, Miss Baxter. *(Puts cape around her.)* The—the young man is hanging around again.

Beulah. What young man? Not that—same one?

Weller. Yes.

Beulah. He's going to drive me crazy—— *(Cross to* R.C.*..)* I've been telling them for a week to get rid of him. Why, it's been over a week.

Weller. *(Nods)* Since the picture began.

Beulah. He's beginning to get on my nerves. Following me every place. *(Sit on bench* L.C.*)*

59

WELLER. Perhaps if *you* would *speak* to him once—tell him to go away——

BEULAH. *(Sits)* I certainly will. Ah—where is he?

WELLER. Why—here he is.

BEULAH. Oh, young man! Come here.

(MERTON *enter* L.I.)

MERTON. *(Eagerly)* Yes, Miss Baxter?

BEULAH. You've been following me around for a week, and now it *must stop*.

MERTON. But I—I haven't. All I wanted was—

BEULAH. What *do* you want? That's just what I'd like to know.

MERTON. Oh, I—I only thought if you'd just let me be around—— (WELLER *exit* L.I.)

BEULAH. Oh! . . .

MERTON. *(Crosses* R.*)* Are you going to do the scene on the ship tonight?

BEULAH. I suppose so. But tell me, you've seen me in my pictures, is that it?

MERTON. Oh, yes. And I've *admired* you, Miss Baxter—and I think you're wonderful.

BEULAH. *(Pleased)* You don't say so.

MERTON. You're—you're my ideal—practically.

BEULAH. Really? Won't you sit down?

MERTON. *(Sits)* Do you remember—when you made that personal appearance—in Peoria? I don't suppose you saw me—I was right in the front row, though—and I was the one that—opened the door of your automobile, afterward.

BEULAH. You did? *(Laughs.)*

MERTON. Yes. Of course I wouldn't expect you to remember—me. It was May 19th.

BEULAH. And you . . . you've been following me because you——

MERTON. Well, it's because I just wanted to see

you—actually taking a picture—— *(Rise.)* And especially here on the ship—*(Cross* R.C.*)*—and I thought, maybe, if there was ever——

(ROSENBLATT *enters* L.I.)

ROSENBLATT. All right—come on, let's get at this. And, Beulah, you get out—you only interrupt me!

BEULAH. Is that so? *(Rise.)*

ROSENBLATT. Yes, *it is!* I'd have been finished long ago if you hadn't bothered me all the time.

BEULAH. *(R.)* It isn't my fault if you always do things wrong.

ROSENBLATT. *(L.)* Now, what do you mean by that?

BEULAH. Exactly what I say. There hasn't been a thing all week——

ROSENBLATT. Oh, for God's sake, *shut up*——

MERTON. *(Unable to stand it any longer)* I beg your pardon, but you're forgetting yourself.

ROSENBLATT. What—what's that?

MERTON. You forget that there are ladies present—and I must insist that you apologize.

(BEULAH *breaks into laughter.*)

ROSENBLATT. Apologize? *(To* MERTON*)* For God's sake, get away from here! Get out! I've got enough trouble without you! Get out!

MERTON. All right, but be careful how you treat this lady—because I'm not going far—— *(Exit* L. ROSENBLATT *follows and looks after him.* BEULAH *laughs.)*

ROSENBLATT. Well, well, I'll be—well— (BEULAH *laughs again.)* Come on, we'll take this ship scene and then we're through for the night. Where's that girl? Come, you people—come on——

(The GIRL *and* MONTAGUE *enters from* R. *stage.)*

GIRL.   We're coming, Commander.

ROSENBLATT.   Well, hurry up.   Now we're going to shoot the jump, and——

BEULAH.   *(Rise)*   Please make it clear to her that it must be a very high dive.   My reputation is at stake.

ROSENBLATT.   All right, all right.

BEULAH.   She'll have to do better than she did in the tenement jump.   Why, I'd have been ashamed to do a jump like that.

GIRL.   Oh, everybody knows you'd be ashamed to do any kind of a jump, Miss Baxter.   *(Goes up on boat.)*

BEULAH.   What's that?

ROSENBLATT.   Now, now!   Come back here and sit down!   (GIRL *goes to boat and gets in it.)*   Now, what we've got to get here is action.   *(To* MONTAGUE.)*   Now, when you come out there with the gun I want you to pretty near fall off the boat a couple of times.

MONTAGUE.   Mr. Rosenblatt—since giving my services to the motion pictures, I have been killed in a great many ways——

ROSENBLATT.   And——

MONTAGUE.   And generally very early in the story.

ROSENBLATT.   Now we'll shoot this one scene and then we're through for the night.

BEULAH.   Well, I, for one, shall not remain.   You will have to get on as well as you can without me. I never could stand night work.   *(Exit.)*

ROSENBLATT.   Oh, you make me sick, Beulah. Now come on, people—let's get this.   And put some guts into it, and for God's sake, Harry, watch your camera line——   *(Exit* L.2.)*

MONTAGUE.   *Guts!*   And to think that the Mon-

tagues were actors when the Rosenblatts were just
Rosenblatts—— *(Goes up—gets on boat.* ROSEN-
BLATT *enter* L.)

ROSENBLATT. Now make it snappy. *(Walks out
of sight.)*

GIRL. *(On the boat)* All right, Commander, but
it's certainly not what I'd call a quiet evening with
my books.

(BAIRD *enters* L.)

BAIRD. Hello, kid.

GIRL. Hello, Jeff. Still waiting.

BAIRD. *(To* ROSENBLATT, *who enters* L.) Hello,
Rosie.

ROSENBLATT. How are you, Baird? *(To the*
GIRL) Now I'm going to catch this from over here
—and we're going to see if we can't get it right.
Remember, Miss Baxter.

GIRL. I'll never forget her. Will you?

ROSENBLATT. Well, let's all try! *(As he exits* L.)

BAIRD. Still at it, eh?

GIRL. Sure, you know Rosenblatt, but don't go
far—I'll only be ten minutes—then I'll belong to the
ages—— Oh, Weller—— (WELLER *enters and
she throws him her blanket.* WELLER *goes up* L.)

ROSENBLATT. All right, Montague.

GIRL. All right—— *(She hands the blanket back
to* WELLER—*turns to* JEFF.) It's a nice little game,
Jeff, and what makes it especially good are the lovely
people *in* it. *(Throw blanket to* JEFF. *Exit* R. *into
boat.)*

ROSENBLATT. *(From off* R. *as* BAIRD *stands looking after the girl)* And make it snappy!

(The lights change. BAIRD, *whistling idly, starts to
stroll across toward* L. *again. About* C. *he en-*

counters WELLER *and peers at him in the semi-darkness.)*

BAIRD. Hello, Weller.
WELLER. Hello, Mr. Baird.
BAIRD. Tough night, eh?
WELLER. Certainly is.

(BAIRD *resumes his whistling and strolls off at* L.)

ROSENBLATT. *(Off* R.) Now! Let's get it right this time. Ready, back there?
MONTAGUE. *(From rear)* Ready!
ROSENBLATT. All right, lights, let's have the rain —come on with the rain! Good! Action! Camera——

(The MONTAGUE GIRL *steals fearsomely out of the cabin. Just as she appears,* MERTON *strolls on at* L. *down stage. "Strolls" is not quite the word, for there is nothing debonaire about him just at present. He has been sleeping on the lot for a week, most of the time in his clothes. He has not shaved for four days, nor eaten for two. The result of his starvation is that his thoughts are jumbled and confused, and most likely to pour forth irrelevantly. He is, in fact, almost on the edge of delirium.)*

MERTON. *(To* WELLER, *after watching for a second)* Gee, she is doing the ship scene, isn't she?
WELLER. Huh?
MERTON. I just want to feast my eyes on her— the wonder woman of the silver screen.
ROSENBLATT. Come on—come on—along that rail—keep in the camera—I want your face—come on, Montague—keep in the lightning flashes—action; action; now you see her, Montague—get ready to

jump—— *(As the* GIRL *swings to the rope and jumps,* MONTAGUE *fires.)*

MERTON. *(Just before she jumps)* She's going to jump.

MONTAGUE. *(After he has fired)* Ha, ha, ha——

MERTON. Gosh!

ROSENBLATT. All right, let it go at that; throw on the guide lights, Tom—knock off till morning—— *(Effects are thrown off and the rain stops.)*

MERTON. Gee! she's coming up right here.

WELLER. Sure she is.

MERTON. Gosh!

*(*MERTON *falls back a few steps, awe-stricken. There is a pause, then the* MONTAGUE GIRL *climbs up out of the water.* WELLER *throws the coat over her just as before.)*

GIRL. *(Not seeing* MERTON *at first)* Yes, sir! The bird that said they'd heated the water was just an ordinary liar!

MERTON. *(Swept off his feet)* Wh-wh-what?

GIRL. *(Peering at him)* Hello, trouper. *(There is both surprise and concern in her voice.)* Haven't seen you for a long time. How's everything—all jake?

MERTON. Why—why—— *(He looks into the water)*—how do you come to—— Isn't Beulah Baxter——

WELLER. Miss Montague's *doubling* for her. I've been trying to tell you.

GIRL. *(Regretfully)* Weller!

WELLER. *(Dully)* Huh?

MERTON. Why—why—no—no! She doesn't ever have anybody—I heard her say so her own self.

*(*WELLER, *with a shrug, walks out of the circle of light, but does not leave the stage.)*

GIRL. I'm sorry, kid, but it had to come out sooner or later. I don't like to bust up any dreams, but I've been doubling for her all along.

MERTON. *(Nearly hysterical)* No—she wouldn't do it! I don't believe it! Why, she's the most wonderful—— *(He grows incoherent)* I don't think—Gashwiler——

GIRL. Take it easy, trouper. And—ah—let me take a look at you. You know, I haven't seen you for a week. (MERTON *makes no move to come closer. She peers at him.)* Sure everything's jake? (MERTON *nods, unable to answer.)* Had any work since—that one we did together? *(No answer.)* Come on, kid—let's hear.

MERTON. *(With difficulty)* I—I've been all right. *(Desperately)* I've really got to get back—on—location. *(He starts to go.)*

GIRL. Hold on! Don't hurry. If you go, *I'll* be all alone. *(He pauses—the* GIRL *turns to* WELLER.) Oh, Mr. Weller.

WELLER. *(From the darkness)* Yes, Miss Montague.

GIRL. Would you mind running over and getting two cups of coffee and about four of those sandwiches?

WELLER. Right! *(He disappears at* L.)

MERTON. Not—anything for me, thank you.

GIRL. Oh, I know—that's for Weller and me.

MERTON. So then if you don't mind I'll be getting back.

GIRL. Don't run away. Come on over here where I can see you. *(He comes reluctantly.)* That's the stuff. Take a seat. *(He sits on an upturned box. She looks at him closely.)* What makes you look like that?

MERTON. I—we were taking miner stuff, and—

GIRL. Miner stuff?

MERTON. *(Suddenly conscious of his appearance)*

That's the reason I—— *(His hand goes to his chin)* —raised a garden. *(The word comes strangely from him. He is but imitating her.)* I've got to get back. *(He rises—the note of hysteria is again in his voice.)*

GIRL. *(In cool tones of command, presses him down again)* You're not going yet, trouper. *(A pause.)* You know you've got to *learn to face the music.*

MERTON. *(His resistance wearing down)* Yes?

GIRL. You've had a little dream go back on you to-night, and you're sort of broken up. But as long as things have gone that far you might as well hear the rest of it.

MERTON. *(Irrelevantly)* She said she was keeping faith with her public.

GIRL. They all say it. In the first place, Sig Rosenblatt—— *(MERTON looks up. The GIRL proceeds gently)*—well, he's her husband.

MERTON. That—director?

GIRL. And that ain't all. He's her fourth—since she began courting.

MERTON. *(Dully)* He's her—husband? Beulah Baxter is—Mrs. Rosenblatt?

GIRL. *(Sympathetically)* That's right.

MERTON. And you've been—doubling for her?

GIRL. That's right.

MERTON. But—where she rode across the canyon in a bucket—*(The GIRL nods)*—and drove her automobile off the bridge—*(Another nod)*—and crept along the side of that building——

GIRL. *(Nods)* All little Eva.

MERTON. *(Completely crushed)* Oh, my God!

(WELLER appears with coffee and sandwiches.)

GIRL. Here we are! *(Cross to WELLER.)*

WELLER. *(Casually)* Have a sandwich, trouper?

MERTON. *(Rises, cross R., scoring the dramatic*

triumph of his life) No, thanks, I couldn't eat a mouthful. (WELLER *disappears again into the darkness.)*

GIRL. *(With determination this time)* Sit down. *(He does so.)* It was a grand performance, kid, but it didn't fool mother for a minute. *(For reply* MERTON *shivers and averts his gaze.)* Have a sandwich. *(This time* MERTON *takes the sandwich. He eats it voraciously—in about three bites. No word is spoken —but when the sandwich is finished the* GIRL *simply hands him another.)* Hey! Slow up for the curves. *(It goes like the first—still without a word. He seems to expect a third.)* You've got to start in easy. Have some coffee? *(He takes it. He calms down a little.)* When did you eat last? *(She sits.)*

MERTON. *(In a whisper)* I can't remember.

GIRL. *(Looking at his clothes)* You haven't been home? *(She drinks coffee.)*

MERTON. *(Beginning to find himself)* I—I didn't have any money—except what I got that one day.

GIRL. With Crusoe?

MERTON. *(Nods)* It lasted till—a couple of days ago.

GIRL. *(Puzzled)* But if you didn't go home——

MERTON. I—I been right on the lot.

GIRL. For a week?

MERTON. *(Another nod)* I was afraid if I went out—I couldn't get back on again. So I—I found a cabin they'd put up, and—there was a bed in it, and then when they tore that down, after the fight, why, there was a picture where a girl was told to come home—her mother was dying, and I waited, and pretty soon they showed the mother and she was in bed. That night, after they'd all gone, I—slept there.

GIRL. *(Shaking her head)* Well, you're certainly

made out of the stuff that gets there—— *(She breaks off.)* Where'd you come from?

MERTON. Simsbury, Illinois. I worked in a store there.

GIRL. I see.

MERTON. But I always wanted to be a picture actor. I used to go to see— *(His voice changes)*— Beulah—Baxter—whenever they showed one of her pictures—and—Harold Parmalee, and all of them. And I read where they were trying to do something bigger and finer, and I thought if *I* came out here— well, it's worth sacrificing to do something worth while—don't you think?

GIRL. *(With an excited nod)* Go on. Don't ask *me* anything.

MERTON. So I saved up two hundred and seventy dollars, and while I was doing it I practiced acting all I could.

GIRL. How did you practice?

MERTON. *(Digging a document from his pocket)* Well, well, you see, this is it! It's the *Film Incorporation Bureau's* course—see, it certifies, right there——

GIRL. *(Examining it)* A course in acting?

MERTON. Yes.

GIRL. *(Still looking at it)* Stebbensville, Kansas.

MERTON. That's where their main school is, but then they can tell if you're talented, because they send you a list of questions, and then if you don't answer them right, why, they won't accept you, but if you do, then they let you have the course.

GIRL. And you answered them *all* right?

MERTON. They—they said my answers showed unusual talents. Then besides, I—I send them my art studies—*(He delves into his pocket)*—you see, showing me as different characters—— *(Hands pictures to girl.)*

GIRL. *(Half to herself, as she takes them)* For God's sake!

MERTON. *(Looking at them with her)* You see, that's—that's me as Two-Gun Benson, there.

GIRL. *(Her eyes beginning to light up)* Saying good-bye to the horse!

MERTON. Yes—you know that scene——

GIRL. Do I? I've raised horses *for* it.

MERTON. And then here I am for society dramas. I mean where the girl's father is a power in Wall Street—like that one where—— *(Indicating photo.)*

GIRL. *(Rises, still more excited as she inspects this photograph)* What a minute! Kid, this one is great—positively great!

MERTON. *(Pleased)* Do you think so?

GIRL. "Yours truly, Clifford Armytage," but— *(She looks from MERTON to the photograph)*—there's —there's something here I can't put my finger on it, it—it reminds me of somebody. *(MERTON pleased, waits for her to guess.)* Somebody I've seen lately —somebody that—I've got it! Harold Parmalee!

MERTON. *(Rises)* I hoped you'd notice it! That's what I want to do if I am—like he does— really serious things that—that will help to uplift the screen art—I mean big things in a really big way, and——

GIRL. *(Looking at him as though transfixed)* Kid!

MERTON. Yes?

GIRL. Turn your face that way! *(He does so.)* Now toward me again! *(MERTON does so.)* It's great—positively great—even with the lace you can't miss it! *(Cross R.C.)*

MERTON. Huh!

GIRL. *(Intensely excited)* Trouper! *(She whisks out some bills from around neck.)* I want you to take this and go home and get all cleaned up and some food inside of you and come back and meet me here at eight o'clock in the morning. Got that straight?

MERTON. Oh, I couldn't accept——

GIRL. I'm only lending it to you, and you're going to pay me back. You're going to be a big success—I got something all planned out. God help me. *(Cross* L.C. *This last is in lowered voice.)*

BAIRD. *(From off* L.*)* How are you coming, Kid?

GIRL. Don't go away, Jeff—just the guy I want, Weller! Oh, Weller!

(WELLER appearing, enters L.2 *entrance.)*

WELLER. Yes, Miss Montague.

GIRL. Weller, I want you to go with this trouper here—— *(She turns to* MERTON.*)* What's your name?

MERTON. *(After a second's hesitation)* Clifford Armytage.

GIRL. Your name, not your residence.

MERTON. *(Glad to get it out)* Merton Gill.

GIRL. That's better. *(*JEFF BAIRD *enters* L.3 *entrance, cross to* C. *Back to* WELLER.*)* I want you to travel along with Merton here while he goes home and gets cleaned up. *(To* MERTON*)* Do you remember where you live?

MERTON. Yes, but I don't——

GIRL. That's enough! *(Back to* WELLER.*)* Then take him to a restaurant and feed him till he cries for help! Get that?

WELLER. *(Catching her excitement)* Yes!

GIRL. After that, go back home with him and don't leave him! Get this straight—sit up with him all night if necessary and see that he's on this spot at nine o'clock tomorrow morning!

(WELLER gets MERTON—takes him off.)

MERTON. *(As* WELLER *starts to take him off toward* R.*)* But—I—I—don't want to——

GIRL. And if you don't go right away I'll come along myself. (WELLER *and* MERTON *disappear at* L.*)* Jeff, I've found a million dollars for you!

BAIRD. *(With a half-turn away)* It's yours. *(Starting* R.*)*

GIRL. *(Grabbing him)* No, get this! He's a galloot that came here from Cranberry or some place to be an actor! He took an acting course by correspondence and got a lot of photographs taken! Here they are! *(She passes them over.)* Who's he look like?

BAIRD. Good Lord!

GIRL. A dead ringer!

BAIRD. But what are you going to do about it?

GIRL. Don't you see? He looks like Parmalee and he wants to do Parmalee stuff! All right, put him in a Buckeye comedy, and let him kid the life out of Parmalee! Only don't tell him he's supposed to be funny.

BAIRD. *(Letting it dawn on him slowly, looks at the photographs again)* It looks wonderful, but can we put it over?

GIRL. Yes, but not if he knows it's a comedy. He hates comedies.

BAIRD. It's taking an awful chance.

GIRL. We can fix it easy.

BAIRD. *(Almost unable to believe it—another look at the photos)* But it's a bear of an idea. You're sure he doesn't know he's funny?

GIRL. He doesn't know anything's funny. You've got to put him absolutely serious in one of those screams of yours with Bert Chester's cross-eyes and he'll be immense!

BAIRD. But suppose he finds out?

GIRL. That's the only thing I'm afraid of. We've got to keep it from him for a while, that's all. He's got a trusting way of looking at you that's sort of got me, Jeff, and if he ever finds out I did it, I couldn't stand it. He's a nice kid, but he certainly looks like the second plume on a hearse.

BAIRD. *(Noticing* MERTON, *who has returned with* WELLER*)* Psst!

GIRL. *(In a quick, tense undertone)* Do you think he heard?

BAIRD. *(In the same tone)* I'm not sure.

MERTON. I—I didn't remember if I'd—that is— I came back to thank you for——

GIRL. Oh, that's all right. You remember Mr. Baird, don't you—Jeff Baird? *(Crosses* MERTON'S L. *Backs up to* L.*)*

BAIRD. How are you, Kid?

MERTON. Oh, yes.

BAIRD. Well, you're going to *work* for me, now.

MERTON. What?

GIRL. Surest thing you know.

BAIRD. I'm going to give you a *real* chance and in *real* pictures.

MERTON. But he—he only makes—comedies.

GIRL. Comedies? I should say not! Why, he's—

BAIRD. Well, I used to make comedies, but I'm through with them. From now on I'm going to make serious pictures.

MERTON. Serious pictures? *(To the* GIRL*)* Is he—honestly?

GIRL. Why—yes.

BAIRD. Of course I may make a comedy once in a while, but I'm anxious to enter a bigger field.

MERTON. Oh, I'm awfully glad. You're sure you mean—regular serious ones?

BAIRD. Yes, indeed!

MERTON. Significant—I mean?

BAIRD. That's the word, exactly.

MERTON. And—and you want me to—come with you?

BAIRD. You bet I do! You've had a wonderful recommendation. *(He glances at the photos.)*

MERTON. *(To the* GIRL*)* You did it! You did it all! It's everything I ever hoped for. It's my great opportunity. I've always dreamed about it. And now you've made it possible. You've opened the door for me.

GIRL. *(More than willing not to be thanked)* That's all right.

MERTON. *(Back to* BAIRD*)* And—and Mr. Baird, too! You're going to make serious pictures at last. I—I'm awfully glad to hear that. *(He shakes* BAIRD's *hand.)* I'll give you of my best, my very best, and *oh!* I certainly congratulate you, Mr. Baird —I certainly congratulate you!

CURTAIN

ACT IV

Scene I

Scene: *The office of* Jeff Baird, *the Buckeye Comedy King. Desk and two chairs center. Film cutting table* r. *Center wicker table* l.c. *on walls. Three sheets of Buckeye Comedies. Photograph of film beauties, etc.*

Weller *and* Baird *discovered at rise, sitting on desk* c. *Laugh at rise.*

Baird. *(Speaking as curtain rises)* So then 1 says you take aim in the mirror and shoot this guy over your shoulder. Only it reverses in the picture he says, so what you must do to make it come out right is to shoot straight into the mirror. Yes, says the kid, but won't that break the mirror? I says yes, but it'll come out all right in the picture.

Weller. And Armytage believed you?

Baird. Sure he did. He certainly is the prize sap.

Weller. And you got two whole pictures out of him without his tumbling?

Baird. Pretty near now. Flips and I have worked it smooth. Every time he gets suspicious— we kid him along—he's easy that way.

Weller. *(Rises)* Gee, that's too good to keep!

Baird. Now don't try to put anything over on me. It's all right, here in the office, but you and Davy Gripple have got to watch out when the kid's around.

Weller. I don't know what you're——

Baird. Oh, yes, you do. Now, I'm telling you and you can tell Davy for me, that I don't want any

75

of the bunch to laugh at the kid while we're shooting this scene.

WELLER.   What do you mean?

BAIRD.   Tell him no alibis.   I saw Davy laughing his head off when we were shooting that rescue stuff this morning.

WELLER.   Maybe he couldn't help it.

BAIRD.   Well, we've all played the game so far and he hasn't got wise yet.   And there's no reason why we can't finish up this second picture before he tumbles.   *(Goes to cutting machine.)*   Here's the other half of the fight.

WELLER.   *(Crosses* R., *to* BAIRD)   Is that it?

BAIRD.   Yah.   Here's where he knocks the screen off the free lunch.   We'll leave it just like that and put in that piece where the cheese jumps up and bites the bartender.

WELLER.   And then back into the fight again?

BAIRD.   That's right.   About ten feet and then mark it for a chemical fade-out.

WELLER.   Then are you going to fade into the captions?

BAIRD.   No.   There's my sequence just where it's marked.   Use your skull.

WELLER.   You must have changed it.

BAIRD.   I know I did.   Don't worry, Weller.   It'll be smoother and quicker into the laugh.   We can jump back outside the saloon again and show him putting on his spurs.

WELLER.   But you haven't got that piece?

BAIRD.   I know we haven't—lovey, and that's why we're doing a retake.

WELLER.   But if you——

(MONTAGUE GIRL *enters* L.I.)

GIRL.   Hello, Jeff.

BAIRD.   Hello.

GIRL. Jeff, could I see you alone for a minute?

BAIRD. Sure. Weller, take that new Number Six title over to Jackson.

WELLER. Sure. *(Exits with title card.)*

BAIRD. What's the matter, kid?

GIRL. He's outside there. Ready for that close-up of the spurs.

BAIRD. Fine. When we get that the first picture's *all washed up*.

GIRL. And I was wondering——

BAIRD. What?

GIRL. Do you have to take that scene again, Jeff?

BAIRD. Now don't worry. I told him it was just so we could get a close-up of the spurs. Then we can work it in as a flash when they throw him out of the saloon.

GIRL. I'm scared, Jeff. More than I was at first, even.

BAIRD. It's a cinch.

GIRL. Maybe it is. But I'm scared, anyway.

BAIRD. *(Back of desk)* What's the matter with you? There's no danger. He still thinks he's playing in a serious Parmalee drama, and if you told him it was a Buckeye Comedy he wouldn't believe you.

GIRL. *(c.)* I just watched him out there, waiting. I never felt so guilty in my life. He was so trustful, Jeff. He really believes in his heart he's doing a big, vital drama and——

BAIRD. He's getting good money and you've saved his life.

GIRL. I'm wondering whether anybody could have forced him to take that money if he'd known what he was doing. When I think of him coming all the way out here to Hollywood, so innocent he doesn't know a close-up from a censor; and of our making a Buckeye comedy out of him without him knowing it——

BAIRD.   Say, you're not getting emotional, are you?

GIRL.   What?

BAIRD.   I say, you're not falling for this kid?

GIRL.   I don't know.   What do you think?

BAIRD.   I don't know—yet.

GIRL.   If you find out, I wish you'd tell me.   I never felt this way before.   You know, he came out here with a lot of ideals and he's lost one or two of them already.   And when I think of that look in his eyes——

BAIRD.   Still, he's got to find out some day—hasn't he?

GIRL.   I suppose so.

BAIRD.   Well, then let nature take its course. *(Crosses R.)*

GIRL.   I wonder just what that'll be, Jeff.   Is it going to knock him out, or will he bounce?   And I was also kind of wondering whether he'd ever speak to me again. *(Pause, then brightly)*   Oh, well! You're ready for the kid now, huh?

BAIRD.   Sure.   Let him come in.

GIRL.   *(Opening the door)*   All right, Merton—Merton! (GIRL *exits.*)

(MERTON *enters, wearing chaps, sombrero and spurs.*)

BAIRD.   Well?

MERTON.   *(Sits L. of table)*   Mr. Baird, there's something I want to—talk to you about.

BAIRD.   Sure.

MERTON.   I—I don't like to say anything about anybody that isn't fair, Mr. Baird, but——

BAIRD.   I want to hear any complaints, Merton.

MERTON.   Well, it's—Mr. Bert Chester.

BAIRD. Yes?

MERTON. Yes. I think he's taking his work pretty lightly, Mr. Baird.

BAIRD. How do you mean, Merton?

MERTON. Well, inasmuch as you let him keep on acting in spite of his cross-eyes—I mean, because of his sick mother, and all that—I don't think he ought to laugh when people are doing serious work.

BAIRD. Oh, you mean this morning? For a minute *I* thought he was laughing, too. Then I saw it was just an old lip trouble he's had for years. It's a sort of nervous tickling he gets. He apologised to me and asked me to apologise to you. I guess he was afraid you'd laugh at him—he *is* kind of ridiculous, with all his ailments.

MERTON. I wouldn't have laughed.

BAIRD. No, I know you wouldn't. But he's just terribly sensitive. However, if you want me to——

MERTON. Oh, no. I wouldn't hurt his feelings—for worlds.

BAIRD. Don't let it worry you any more, then.

MERTON. But while we're on the subject, Mr. Baird——

BAIRD. Yes?

MERTON. I think I ought to have a little better support in my—next picture.

BAIRD. Oh, better support, eh?

MERTON. Yes. And—ah—I think it's time for me to do something different from Harold Parmalee. I wouldn't want the public to—ah——

BAIRD. Oh, sure, you're right.

MERTON. Besides, I was watching one of Parmalee's picture the other day, and—I don't think he's quite as good as he used to be, Mr. Baird.

BAIRD. That so?

MERTON. Yes. Of course it may just be that my viewpoint is changing, but I think he's falling off a little.   Mind you, I think he's still good, but——

(Enter ROSENBLATT.)

ROSENBLATT.   Excuse me.   *(Crosses* R. *to* BAIRD.)
MERTON.   Excuse me, Mr. Rosenblatt.
ROSENBLATT.   Yes, yes.   *(To* BAIRD) Kerrigan
says you want that other projection room at nine
o'clock, Baird.   Do you think that's fair?
BAIRD.   It's fair if I send in my notice first.
ROSENBLATT.   You ought to know *I'm* cutting
"Mother of the World" right now.   You ought to
know as a gentleman that I need that room every
spare minute——
BAIRD.   Well, calm down and I'll tell you some-
thing.   I'll be through with it at nine-fifteen.
ROSENBLATT.   Oh, why didn't they say so?   They
told me you wanted it till midnight.
BAIRD.   Well, I don't.
ROSENBLATT.   *(Crosses to door*—MERTON *there)*
Well, thanks very much, old man.   I had no idea—
(Meets MERTON.)
MERTON.   Hello, Mr. Rosenblatt.
ROSENBLATT.   *(Vaguely)*   Oh, how are you?
MERTON.   I guess you don't remember me, do
you?
ROSENBLATT.   No, I don't believe I do.
MERTON.   Merton Gill.   *(Recalling)*   Oh—Clif-
ford Armytage.
ROSENBLATT.   *(Snaps fingers)*   Gill—Armytage.
H'm, why, no, I can't say that I do remember just—
ah——
MERTON.   A couple of months ago, when you
were starting on "Robinson Crusoe"?   *(A pause.)*
Remember—you fired me from the scene in the li-
brary?   (BAIRD *is nervous—crosses* R.)
ROSENBLATT.   *(Still vaguely)*   Oh, yes, I think I
do recall——

MERTON. Gee, I've often thought of that, Mr. Rosenblatt. That was one of my earlier struggles, all right. You must have thought I was pretty green that day, when I didn't know how to walk down to the camera or anything. I guess I *was* pretty green.

ROSENBLATT. *(More definitely)* Yes, yes—I remember. What are you doing now?

MERTON. Why, I'm—— *(He stops, modestly.)*

BAIRD. *(Quickly)* He's with me now.

ROSENBLATT. Oh!

BAIRD. I'm going to feature him. *(Motion to* ROSENBLATT *not to give joke away.)*

ROSENBLATT. *(To* MERTON) Oh, yes, I heard about you.

BAIRD. *(Nervously)* Well—let's get after that retake. *(Starts for door* R.)

MERTON. Just a minute, Mr. Rosenblatt. *(With a light laugh)* Those were great times you and I had together, Mr. Rosenblatt. I guess you'll never forget how terrible I was.

ROSENBLATT. *(Who has forgotten long ago)* Oh, I don't know.

BAIRD. *(Anxious to get rid of him)* Waiting for you, kid. *(Opens door.)*

MERTON. Yes, sir. *(Crosses* R., *then turns to* ROSENBLATT, *hand on shoulder. He gives a long, retrospective sigh.)* Some day—some day you and I will have many a good laugh over those days, Mr. Rosenblatt. Very glad you dropped in. So long. *(He goes out, with such dignity as the spurs permit.* BAIRD *and* ROSENBLATT *exchange looks.)*

CURTAIN

ACT IV

Scene II

SCENE: *The living room of* MERTON'S *boarding house. Stairway leading off* L. *masked by wall; two or three steps being visible. Door* C. *leading to another room. Street* D.L. *Window* R.I. *Fireplace with sofa before it,* L.I. *Tables and chairs. Telephone on table* R.C.

MRS. PATTERSON *discovered at 'phone.*

MRS. PATTERSON. Hello, is that you, pa?—No, he ain't in yet. I don't know what's happened to him. *(Crosses to table* L.C.*)* He's not in his room! I knocked three times, and then went in. I tell you he ain't been in at all. His bed ain't been slept in. *(A pause.)* I bet they went and gave him a big party, celebrating the success of the picture. Now, I'm sorry about that. I hope he don't go and dissipate, just because he made a big hit last night. My, but he was funny, though. Them spurs . . . Yes, all right. Good-bye, pa. *(Hangs up—starts to stairs. 'Phone. Crosses right to 'phone—at 'phone)* Hello . . . Oh, hello, Miss Montague.—He ain't here.—I thought maybe you knew.—Huh?—No, I mean he wasn't here all night. Ain't that funny, after his picture making such a big hit? Oh, I should say he *was* there. And funny! I don't remember when I've laughed so much. Didn't *you* think it was funny? Well, he certainly is entitled to it if anybody ever was. Did you see the write-ups the paper gave him? He certainly made an awful big success. *(Meditatively)* Out all night. It just shows how success goes to a person's head. You're wor-

82

ried sick, I can tell the way you talk. Yes, I will. Good-bye. *(Hangs up and exits up* C.)

(There is a considerable pause, then WELLER *appears. He turns back to look at someone behind him.)*

WELLER. *(Entering* R.1E.—*wearily)* Come on—you've come this far. (MERTON *appears.)* Now, will you stay here till I get Miss Montague?

MERTON. I suppose so. *(Sits.)*

WELLER. You ought to eat some breakfast.

MERTON. Food!

WELLER. Or go to bed or something.

MERTON. Bed!

WELLER. Well, anyhow, I got you home.

MERTON. *(Dully)* Ya. *(Pause.)* Thanks, Weller. Thanks for—walking around all night, and—sitting in the park and everything.

WELLER. Oh, that's all right. Good-night.

MERTON. *(Breaking out again—rises)* The shame of it! The shame of it all! *(Crosses* L.)

WELLER. Haven't I been telling you there ain't any shame in it?

MERTON. They shamed me! Shamed me in front of all those people!

WELLER. Good-morning—*(Yawns)*—Mr. Gill. And for the thousandth time, nobody shamed you. You made the biggest hit in the world, and they simply laughed their heads off.

MERTON. You give them the best and finest that's in you, and they laugh! That's a *hit*. Jeff Baird meant it to be funny! So did she!

WELLER. Well, it *was* funny.

MERTON. I'll never trust a woman again.

WELLER. Good-morning. *(Exits* R.1E., *wearily.)*

MERTON. *(Stares into space—sees paper—reads)* "The funniest newcomer in the realm of comedy."

(MERTON *tosses paper aside.* MRS. PATTERSON *enters.*)

MRS. PATTERSON. *Well,* good morning!

MERTON. Good-morning.

MRS. PATTERSON. I'm certainly awfully glad you got home. We were worried about you.

MERTON. I'm—all right.

MRS. PATTERSON. *(Fulsomely)* Congratulations!

MERTON. What?

MRS. PATTERSON. Congratulations!

MERTON. What?

MRS. PATTERSON. Congratulations on your success!

MERTON. Oh!

MRS. PATTERSON. *(Laughs)* My, my! I don't think we ever laughed so much in our lives as we did last night. And I just want to tell you how proud we are of you. (MERTON *starts for stairs.*) Now, can I get you some breakfast?

MERTON. No, thanks. I'm not a bit hungry. *(Exits upstairs.)*

MRS. PATTERSON. *(Calling after him)* If you want any later, I'll be back. I'm just going over to Mrs. Gimble's. *(Knock on door. She goes down to door at* R. *and opens it.* WALBERG, *an agent for the Bigart Film Co., enters.)*

WALBERG. Morning. Mr. Armytage live here?

MRS. PATTERSON. *(Genially)* Mr. Clifford Armytage, I s'pose you mean?

WALBERG. Yes, ma'am.

MRS. PATTERSON. Won't you come in? (WALBERG *crosses to* C. *She closes door—goes to* WALBERG.) Who shall I say's calling, please?

WALBERG. Just tell him there's a gentleman wants to see him on business.

MRS. PATTERSON. *(As engagingly as possible)* You a movie man?

WALBERG. Yes.

MRS. PATTERSON. We saw Mr. Armytage's picture at the Premier last night. We're all very proud about it. My, the way that audience laughed!

WALBERG. *(Pointedly)* Are you *Mrs.* Armytage?

MRS. PATTERSON. Oh, no. Mr. Armytage is a single gentleman. I'm Mrs. J. Emery Patterson. (WALBERG *loses interest in her. There is a pause until his detachment sinks in. She goes to the stairs.)* Well, I'll tell him you're here. *(She apparently is about to call upstairs, but changes her mind.)* Just wait! *(She goes up.)*

(WALBERG *waits patiently. He inspects a picture with the air of a connoisseur, and otherwise occupies himself. In a few moments* MERTON *appears. He wears a dressing-gown. He is very dejected.)*

MERTON. Did you want to see me?

WALBERG. (R.C. *Attempting ingratiation)* Good-morning, Mr. Armytage. I suppose you feel pretty good today.

MERTON. *(After looking him over carefully)* Not so very.

WALBERG. *(Trying to appraise him)* You cer᾿ tainly were a scream last night. (MERTON *gives him a long look, feeling a martyr.)*

MERTON. (L.C.) I suppose Mr. Baird sent you.

WALBERG. (C.) He did not. My name's Walberg, Mr. Armytage, and I'm with the Bigart. I got your address from the Holden office because I thought we ought to have a little talk.

MERTON. I don't want to talk. *(Turns to go.* WALBERG, *laughing it off, motions him to seat.* MERTON *sits* L. *of table.)*

WALBERG. Now, wait! Suppose you let me talk,

then. I've got something that's going to interest you. *(A pause, during which* MERTON, *utterly at sea, tries to guess* WALBERG'S *purpose.)* Won't you sit down? I saw your picture last night, Mr. Armytage. (MERTON *gives a sigh that is half sob.)* Is it definitely certain you're going to stick with Baird?

MERTON. No.

WALBERG. That's fine. *(Sits* R. *of table.* MERTON *again gives him a puzzled look.)* You're new to pictures, I understand?

MERTON. Yes.

WALBERG. Well, don't do like a lot of other comics and try to do straight stuff. You know how far you'd get.

MERTON. I know how far I *got.*

WALBERG. You stick to comedy, because you've got everything. Why, you've got the best low comedy face I've seen in ages. It's got genuine pathos, more pathos than Parmalee, the guy you were kidding. And you've got the gift of the world in knowing just how to kid bad acting. Frankly, I don't believe you could ever make the grade in a serious picture. I candidly don't believe you could register if you imitated a *good* actor. But you've got pathos—pathos and acting, plus. I don't have to tell you that. You and Baird found out your limits and have started you off on what God meant you for.

MERTON. *(Hardly able to stand it)* Mr. Walberg, I——

WALBERG. Now, hold on! Now, there's only one thing the matter with you—*you're too good.* Parmalee makes hokum and the public wants hokum. *You* make satire, which is over the heads of most of the public. Take a beautiful Mormon like Beulah Baxter. She can't act. She probably wouldn't know two and two made four if she didn't get it by gossip. You're different—you've got intelligence. Now, how about doing some stuff for us?

MERTON. You mean—you mean—comedies?

WALBERG. Certainly.

MERTON. *(Decided at last)* I wouldn't think of it.

WALBERG. You mean you wouldn't come with Bigart at all—on any proposition?

MERTON. That's what I mean.

WALBERG. Wouldn't three hundred a week interest you?

MERTON. *(After gulping)* No.

WALBERG. Three fifty?

MERTON. No.

WALBERG. *(Rises, crosses* R., *thinks—pause)* Four hundred!

MERTON. No.

(WALBERG *gets up, takes his hat, looks at* MERTON, *then crosses to the street door.)*

WALBERG. Well, you're a tough egg, but we'll have you with Bigart yet. Yes, sir, even if Mr. Strausheimer has to come here *himself.* Good day. *(Exits* R.I.)

MERTON. *(As* WALBERG *exits)* Good morning. *(He crosses to the fireplace, terribly disturbed.)*

(MRS. PATTERSON *enters, downstairs.)*

MRS. PATTERSON. I'm sorry, but I overheard a little of that gentleman's talk, Mr. Armytage. I must say he seems to feel about you just the same as we feel.

MERTON. *(Rises)* You mean low-comedy face?
                              ('PHONE Ready.)

MRS. PATTERSON. *(Laughs)* Yes, indeed. Why, you were funnier than that cross-eyed man ever was.

MERTON. Thank you. *(Starts up* C. *to stairs.)*

MRS. PATTERSON. Are you going to have another *premeer* soon?

MERTON. *(Horrified)* Yes!

MRS. PATTERSON. I can hardly wait. Now I wish you'd let me get you some breakfast.

MERTON. I don't want any.   *('PHONE.)*

MRS. PATTERSON. It's all ready. *(The telephone bell rings.)* Won't take a second. *(At 'phone.)* Hello. . . . Yes.—Yes, ma'am, he's here now.—If you'll hold the——— What? Oh! Why, he seems to be all right. *(She looks at* MERTON.*)* It's Miss Montague, but she doesn't want to talk to you. *(Into 'phone)* What? Yes, he's terribly happy over it, I guess, though he don't say much. All right, I'll tell him. Yes, m'm. Good-bye. *(Hangs up.)* Miss Montague says she'll be over in a few minutes. *(*MERTON *stands helpless, then starts for the stairs.)* Now, about that breakfast, Mr. Armytage.

MERTON. No! No! And if Miss Montague comes, why—I had to keep an engagement somewhere. *(Exits upstairs.)*

MRS. PATTERSON. H'm! *(She starts for the street door when the knocker sounds. She turns to go to the up-stage door, remembers, and opens the street door.* MR. GASHWILER *enters.)* Yes, sir?

GASHWILER. Good-morning. Is there a Mr. Armytage stopping here. *(He uses a hard "g" and a long "a" in Armytage.)*

MRS. PATTERSON. I suppose you mean Mr. Clifford Armytage.

GASHWILER. Yes, ma'am. Is he home?

MRS. PATTERSON. Yes, sir. *(He enters, she closes door.)* What is the name, please?

GASHWILER. Gashwiler.

MRS. PATTERSON. Mr. Gashwiler?

GASHWILER. Yes, ma'am. He used to work for me.

MRS. PATTERSON. He did?

GASHWILER. In Illinois.

MRS. PATTERSON. And you don't even know his name!

GASHWILER. Well, this Armytage is a kind of a stage name. He was Merton Gill when he worked for me.

MRS. PATTERSON. *(Indicates seat)* Oh, I see. If you'll excuse me, I'll see if he's in. *(She goes to the stairs—collides with MERTON coming down, with hat and coat.)* Oh, I was just going to your room. This gentleman——

MERTON. Mr. Gashwiler!

GASHWILER. Hello, Merton. Well, well, well!

MERTON. *(Deciding on a little swank)* Well, you look fine, Mr. Gashwiler. Oh, I'm terribly glad to see you, Mr. Gashwiler.

GASHWILER. I'm mighty glad to see you, too, Merton.

MRS. PATTERSON. *(With a self-conscious smile)* Well, excuse me—— *(Exits L.)*

MERTON. What are you doing out here?

GASHWILER. Oh, just tourin'. Mrs. Gashwiler and I thought we'd take in the Golden West, and at last here we are. Here for four days, then we go on to San Francisco.

MERTON. I wish I were going with you, Mr. Gashwiler.

GASHWILER. *(Sits L. of table R.)* Well, we'd feel pretty *honored* if you could come, Merton—a great big man like you. Just by a miracle, last night, we seen you in the new picture.

MERTON. *(Panic-stricken—sits R. of table L.)* Did you see it, too?

GASHWILER. I guess I laughed about as much as anyone. Merton, I never knowed what I was talkin' about when I said you hadn't ought every try to get into the movies. Why, you're funnier than anybody

I ever seen. Wait'll we get back to Simsbury. That place is going to have a plate.

MERTON. A what?

GASHWILER. A plate. Yessir. "Here worked Merton Gill." If I have any influence, that town's goin' to honor her illustrious son the way he ought to be honored. I'm goin' to have a brass plate made for the front of the store.

MERTON. No!

GASHWILER. Yes, sir.

MERTON. (*Rises*) Oh, my! (*Pause.*) How's Mrs. Gashwiler? (*Crosses to* GASHWILER—*shakes hands.*)

GASHWILER. Fine. Wants to see you. I was lucky to get your address. Miss Kearns happened to come in the store the day we left and said she had it, so she gave it to me.

MERTON. (*Now a great artist*) Dear old Tessie! How's she getting along?

GASHWILER. Oh, fine, fine! Says she's thinking of comin' out here herself.

MERTON. Yes, she wrote me about that. But I don't think she ought to, Mr. Gashwiler.

GASHWILER. No?

MERTON. No. It's a pretty stiff game, the movies. You've got to have a certain amount of what they call hokum to get your scenarios over. Tessie's an awfully nice girl and all that, but I don't think she could get away with it. It might break her heart. (*Door-knocker heard.*)

GASHWILER. (*Having listened to the oracle*) Well, I'll tell her that.

MERTON. I hope she doesn't try it.

GASHWILER. And now, how about comin' down to the hotel with me and seein' Mrs. Gashwiler? I'll treat you to lunch. (*Door-knocker heard again.*)

MERTON. (*Crosses* R. *to door*) Well, excuse me —I have to—— (*He sees that it is the* GIRL *at the door, but nerves himself to admit her. The* GIRL *enters somewhat timorously.)*

GIRL. *(Scared to death)* Hello!

MERTON. *(Stiffly)* Good-morning. *(Closes door —a pause.)* This is—Miss Montague.

GASHWILER. How do you do—I'm sure.

GIRL. *(Conscious of the tenseness of the situation)* How are—you?

GASHWILER. You in the movies, too?

GIRL. I'm not quite sure just where I am.

GASHWILER. Huh?

GIRL. I was joking. *(Pause.)* Do you—live here?

GASHWILER. No, I'm from Illinois. Merton used to work for me.

GIRL. You're not Mr. Gooseberry, or whatever it is?

GASHWILER. No. Gashwiler's my name.

GIRL. That's it. I remember Gooseberry's the name of the town.

GASHWILER. No, the town's name is Simsbury.

GIRL. I guess my memory's just gone dead.

GASHWILER. Merton a good friend of yours?

GIRL. *(Uncertainly)* We've *seen* a lot of each other. *(Crosses to* L.C.*)*

GASHWILER. Well—— *(Crosses* R. *to* MERTON*)* I hope I see you again.

GIRL. Yes.

GASHWILER. See you later, Merton. Telephone me at the Hollywood.

MERTON. *(Forcing himself to speak)* Yes—I will.

GIRL. *(Not noticing his departure)* Bye-bye!

*(*GASHWILER *exits through street door.* MERTON *regards her for a few moments, then begins speaking cheerily—embarking on a fine piece of acting.)*

MERTON. Well? *(L.C., near table.)*

GIRL. Well? *(C. A pause. Still in doubt.)* You've seen the picture. Shoot.

MERTON. *(Smiling)* All right. I've certainly kidded the life out of all of you.

GIRL. What!

MERTON. I've certainly kidded the whole crowd of you. You thought all along that I thought it was a serious picture, didn't you? You and Baird thought you had me kidded all along, didn't you? Ho, ho! A serious picture with a cross-eyed man doing comedy stuff all around me every minute. I thought it was serious, did I? *Yes, I did!* Like fun! *(Sits.)*

GIRL. Just say some of that again! *(Sits.)*

MERTON. Didn't you people know what I could do and what I couldn't do? Didn't you s'pose I knew as well as anybody that I've got a low-comedy face and that I couldn't make the grade in a serious picture? Of course, I've got real pathos, but anyone can see I couldn't imitate a good actor. Didn't you and Baird ever s'pose I found out my limits and decided to be what God intended me to be? Straight satire—*(Rises)*—that's what I'm doing—and it's over the heads of most of the public. Why, they tell me that I was funnier than that cross-eyed man ever was in his life. And what happens this morning? *(Crosses R.C.)*

GIRL. What happens?

MERTON. Nothing, except that people are coming around to sign me up for four hundred dollars a week. Why, this Bamberger from the Bigart company comes in before I'm really up this morning, asking me if I won't go with his company, and . . . why . . . *(He breaks off as he notices her steady gaze.)*

GIRL. So you know everything, do you? You know you look just too much like Parmalee so that

you're funny? (MERTON *is hit.*) I mean you, that
you look the way Parmalee would if he had brains.

MERTON. Certainly. Parmalee? Why, Parmalee's got nothing but hokum in his pictures, anyway.
Why, anyway, satire—— *(Breaks down and turns.)*

GIRL. Merton! (MERTON *crosses to her and
falls into her arms, sobbing.)* There, don't you
worry! Mother's got you and she's going to never
let you go.

MERTON. *(Sobbing)* It's like that night on the
lot when I found out about you and Beulah Baxter
and you were so——

GIRL. There, there. Don't you worry. Did he
have his poor old mother going for a minute? Yes,
he did. He had her going for a minute, all right.
But he didn't fool her very long, not very long, because he can't ever fool her very long. And he can
bet a lot of money on that.

MERTON. I feel a little better.

GIRL. Of course you do.

MERTON. I didn't see at first how I ever could live
down what I saw last night. I guess I didn't understand, some way. *(He shows he doesn't yet, for that
matter.)*

GIRL. Don't worry, honey. Mother knows what's
what, and she'll tell you all about it in good time.

MERTON. You think I ought to—keep on—making comedies?

GIRL. You will as long as I last. *(There is a
whistle, three sharp blasts, outside.)* That's a friend
of ours. He said he wanted to see you, if you were
feeling . . . well.

MERTON. *(Gaily)* There's nothing the matter
with me. *(Rises. Crosses L. Pause. Second whistle. The GIRL goes to the street door and opens it.
BAIRD's head appears.)*

BAIRD. Is he gunless?

GIRL. I've a pleasant surprise for you. (BAIRD *enters.*)

BAIRD. *(Surveying)* Good-morning, Kid. *(He crosses to* MERTON.*)*

MERTON. *(Smiling)* Well, I guess we did it.

BAIRD. *(Smiles and crosses to shake hands)* I'll say we did. *(Quickly to* GIRL*)* How did *you* do it?

GIRL. Oh, I've got ways.

BAIRD. I got a piece of news at the office that made me come over. You know your picture's a knockout, I suppose?

MERTON. So they tell me.

BAIRD. Yes, and the groundhogs are at work. A mysterious voice called up and got your address this morning. Has anybody been here?

MERTON. Yes, a gentleman from the Bigart dropped in. He wanted to give me a very fine contract. A very fine contract indeed.

BAIRD. Well, don't let those babies tempt you. Remember, you and I have a nice little contract, too, for three years.

MERTON. Oh, I turned him down. I know my place is with you, Mr. Baird. And I want to put everything I can into comedies. I want to give the best that's in me, because I realize that that's where you and God intended me to be.

BAIRD. That's the talk. In three years we'll be giving you a salary that'll knock the eye off the ones Parmalee and those other Swift Premiers get.

MERTON. Still, the public wants that hokum. Why, you take Beulah Baxter, for instance. She's nothing but a high grade Mormon. Why, she wouldn't know two and two was four if she didn't hear people talking. (GIRL *peers at him to see if it can really be* MERTON—*then she gives it up.*)

BAIRD. *(Looks at* GIRL—*crosses* R.*)* Well, I'm off. By the way, the new one looks even better. I'll be glad to show it to you any time—now. Good-bye.

GIRL. Good-bye, Jeff.

BAIRD. He's a nice kid.

GIRL. He's a wonderful kid. (MERTON *hears it.*)

BAIRD. Well, good-bye. (*Goes to door* R. *and opens it.*)

GIRL. Bye-bye——

MERTON. Good-bye.

GIRL. (*Seeing who it is, turns to* MERTON) Kid, you've landed.

MERTON. Say, I haven't had any breakfast yet. Did you eat?

GIRL. I should say not!

MERTON. (*At door* U.L.) Mrs. Patterson! Mrs. Patterson!

MRS. PATTERSON. (*Off stage*) Yes, Mr. Armytage. (*Ready 'phone.*)

MERTON. (*As* MRS. PATTERSON *appears*) I was wondering if there's enough breakfast for two to eat.

MRS. PATTERSON. Indeed, there is. I've kept some things on the stove in case Mr. Armytage changed his mind. He's got to eat a lot to keep himself in condition. (*Starts out.*) Mrs. Gimble wanted to know, and I do, too, whether you'd mind giving us a picture of yourself, autographed. I'd feel very honored. (*The telephone bell rings.* MRS. PATTERSON *answers it.*) Yes, who? Yes, he's here. Just a minute, please.

GIRL. Who is it? (*Stopping* MERTON *by his coat-tail.*)

MRS. PATTERSON. (*Into 'phone*) What is it, please? Oh! Just a minute. (*To the* GIRL) It's the Silver Screenings Magazine. For Mr. Armytage.

MERTON. (*Crossing*) All right. (MRS. PATTERSON *exits.*) Hello! Yes, this is Mr. Armytage.

GIRL. By the way, your name's going to be Merton Gill from now on.

MERTON. *(To her)* Is it? *(She nods.)* Hello, yes. This is Mr. Armytage. That isn't my regular name, though, you know. . . . What? Gill— G, i, l, l. Yes. Merton. . . . That's right. What? Any time you say. If there's anything I can tell the public I'd be very glad to. I don't know what your readers would want to know about me, however. What? I say I don't know what your readers would want to know about me, however. Oh, just hard work, I guess. I've struggled and sacrificed to give the public something—— What? No, I'm not yet, but I think I'm going to be. *(Looks to the GIRL.)* Miss Montague. Yes, that's the lady. Oh, I should say so. More like a pal. And I might also add she's my severest critic.

(MISS MONTAGUE *is standing close to him.)*

CURTAIN

SHEET FOR DIRECTOR TO CAST FROM

MERTON GILL, *Leading Man.*
AMOS G. GASHWILER, *Comedian.*
TESSIE KEARNS *(brunette about thirty-five), Double
    Second Woman.*
MURIEL MERCER *(Blonde, about twenty).*
ELMER HUFF ⎤   *Character Rube.*
         ⎬ *Double*
JEFF BAIRD ⎦   *Comedian.*
SIGMOND ROSENBLATT, *Heavy Man.*
J. LESTER MONTAGUE, *Character Man.*
WELLER, Utility.
CAMERA MAN ⎤
         ⎬ *Double—Utility.*
WALBERG ⎦
HAROLD PARMALEE, *Juvenile.*
BEULAH BAXTER, *Ingenue.*
THE MONTAGUE GIRL, *Leading Woman.*
CASTING DIRECTOR, *about forty* ⎤ *Double—*
                    ⎬ *Character*
MRS. PATTERSON, *about sixty* ⎦ *Woman.*

Can easily be played with seven men, four women,
               six simple sets.
The man who plays Harold Parmalee must be some-
    thing in size and appearance as the man who
    plays Merton.

PROPERTY PLOT

ACT I

Rear room of country store.   Bare stage.
1 small high back desk (not over 3 feet wide).
    Old writing material.
    Paper.
    Ledgers—Desk dressed old ink stand, pens.
1 chair for desk.
2 book shelves.
Shelves filled with
    Shoe boxes, cracker boxes, bolts of dry goods,
       etc.
1 eight by three foot table counter—
    Cloth to cover front.
    Under this a cot with blankets and pillows.
1 old trunk.
1 counter piled with boxes, etc.
1 cheap phonograph (practical).
1 Walter Camp Daily Dozen record.
2 clothes dummies—dressed—1 male, 1 female.
2 signs to hang on same, 10 inches by fourteen.
    (1) on man.   (2) on woman.
     Rainproof   Our Latest
        or   for
  Your Money Back   Milady
                    $6.78

Clothes for dummies:
    Pants and raincoat for man.
    Gingham dress for woman.
Several barrels, dry goods boxes, soap boxes.

Bundle of brooms, shovels, rakes.
Old lawn-mower.
Old scales.
Several flour sacks, filled.
Nest of baskets.
Old wall clock—ten o'clock.
Window shades—small window not practical.
Cigar box on desk—one cigar a performance
1 Magazine—"Shadowland"—on shelf c.
Old black cash box on desk R.
In trunk:
    Revolver in belt and holster.
    Wallet.
    Sombrero.
Clock tick off left.

HAND PROPS.

Merton:
    1 basket filled with 2 packages Uneedas, 2 cans
        tomatoes, 3 filled bags—all off R.2.
Photo, 8x10, man in evening clothes—in trunk.
Correspondence school diploma in large envelope.
Step-ladder.
Gashwiler:
    Bills—$5.
Elmer:
    Package cigarettes.
Tessie:
    1 movie magazine, "Silver Screenings."
    6 photos—postcard size—in envelope.

ACT II

Signs:
        Holden Master
        Picture Corp.
            This sign large enough to cover win-
            dow used L.1 in Act I. 40x40 inches.

Casting
Director
Over window R.C.

No Smoking
Two of these.

Attention Artists
Costumes should be
returned promptly
to Wardrobe Room.

Not responsible for
damage to wardrobe
furnished by artists.

Report any change of
address or telephone
numbers—
Holden Master Picture
Corp.

Blackboard—white letters:
Shooting Schedule
Monday
Tuesday
Wednesday
Thursday
Friday
Saturday

STUDIO
No Admittance
except on order

On door.

Talent Checks
should be cashed
promptly.

Bare stage.
1 eight-foot bench.
2 four-foot benches.
1 small flat-top desk or table.
Writing material.
Several ledgers.
Telephone.
1 swivel chair.
Letter rack with letters on office backing.
Wall calendar.
Several film cans.
Film script (blue back—joined at top like legal paper).
Pad, two by three inches, on desk.
Blue stair carpet to drag on.
Clip board and paper.
Very elaborate watch and chain.
Old Ingersoll watch.
Very large bouquet of roses—with ribbon.
Cane.
Vanity case.
"Billboard."

ACT III—SCENE I

Bare stage.
1 large medallion.
1 small library table and runner.
1 small chair.
1 armchair.
Mantel:
    Dante head.
    2 Italian candlesticks.
    Large painting over mantel.
Moving picture camera with film box on tripod.
Book, "Robinson Crusoe," on table.
Megaphone.

3 folding chairs (one has painted on back, "Mr. Ro-
senblatt").
Whistle.
Slate, with wet sponge and chalk on string—painted:

No.
Scene

Small block of wood—seven-eighths by two by three
painted black—oil—well sand-papered (supposed to be Director's viewing glass).
Small pad, about three by five inches, and pencil.
Sign, eight by twelve inches, to read:

Don't Touch Anything
on This Set.

Reel of fire-hose.

ACT III—Scene II

Floor cloth to catch rice.
Four-foot bench.
Large blanket.
1 kitchen chair.
Off stage R.:
Plate wth two bread and butter sandwiches, cut
very thin, to be eaten quickly.
Two mugs of coffee.

HAND PROPS.

Revolver and blanks—sure-fire.
Correspondence diploma.
3 postcard size photos in envelope. (the duplicates of
those used in Act I—but soiled).
Dollar bills.

ACT IV—Scene I

Desk—writing material—letter basket—books, **etc.**
Desk chair.
2 chairs.
Table to match.
Settee to match.
Hat tree to match.
2 piece awning.
Several large framed pictures of movie actresses for
    wall.
Several film cans.
Film cutter.
Parts of moving picture machine.
Several pieces of film.
2 index cards (as tally cards).
Banner, 3x6—gold letters—black shadows on **red**
    cloth to read:

Buckeye
Comedies
First Prize
Hollywood
Outing
July
30

Tassel on bottom.

ACT IV—Scene II

Boarding house parlor.
Sofa.
4 chairs.
1 armchair.
1 center table—not large—cover.
2 small tables—covers.
Hat rack and umbrella stand.
Irons for fireplace.

Mantel shelf.
2 jardiniers of flowers—poppies.
Shades and lace curtains on rod on window R.1.
On mantel:

> 2 vases of flowers.
> Clock.

Several Los Angeles newspapers.
5 framed pictures—*not* paintings.
1 hanging flower basket of flowers.
Knocker on door R.2.

WARDROBE PLOT

ACT I

MERTON: Old pants and vest—blue shirt, old shoes.
GASHWILER: Business suit without coat. Office
duster.
ELMER HUFF: Sporty light checked suit, white
shoes, straw hat and cane.
TESSIE KEARNS: Black sweater, dark skirt, home-
made hat.

ACT II

MERTON: Grey business suit, not too good a fit, felt
hat, tan shoes.
MONTAGUE GIRL: Red sport coat, white skirt, white
hat, white shoes.
LESTER MONTAGUE: Checked pants, white vest, dark
coat, soft hat, blue tie.
WELLER: Grey pants, white shirt, white shoes.
PARMALEE: Grey pants, white shirt, white shoes.
ROSENBLATT: Riding pants, puttees, white shirt.
JEFF BAIRD: Brown business suit.
CAMERA MAN: White shirt, riding pants, puttees,
light cap.

BEULAH BAXTER: Smart, up-to-date ultra afternoon gown, walking stick.

ACT III—SCENE I

MERTON: Dinner suit—Tuxedo.
MONTAGUE GIRL: Evening gown.
ROSENBLATT: Same as Act II.
WELLER: Same as Act II.
PARMALEE: Dinner suit—Tuxedo—dressing gown.
VIOLINIST: Dark business suit.
CAMERA MAN: Riding pants, puttees, cap.

ACT III—SCENE II

MERTON: Old blue coat, old white pants.
* MONTAGUE GIRL: Sailor suit.
LESTER MONTAGUE: Oilskin coat, pants and hat.
* BEULAH BAXTER: Sailor suit.
ROSENBLATT: Same as Act II.
JEFF BAIRD: Same as Act II.
    * Exactly alike.

ACT IV—SCENE I

MERTON: Cowboy costume complete with two guns and exceptionally large spurs.
MONTAGUE GIRL: Gingham house dress.
JEFF BAIRD: Same as Act II, without coat, cap.
ROSENBLATT: Grey pants, white shirt.
WELLER: Same as Act II.

ACT IV—SCENE II

MERTON: Neat blue suit and straw hat; flannel bathrobe.
JEFF BAIRD: Grey suit—straw hat.
GASHWILER: Business suit—straw hat.

MONTAGUE GIRL: White dress and hat, white shoes.
WALBERG: Neat grey business suit, cane, brown
    derby.
MRS. PATTERSON: Gingham house dress; gingham
    apron.

PROPERTY PLOT

ACT I—COUNTRY STORE

Back shelves for display of goods—grocery store.
1 counter, tables, bolts of dry goods and shoes.
1 chair.
Boxes, barrels, baskets, anything and everything to
    make up a general store.
1 Man dummy.
1 Woman dummy.
1 Showcase.
1 Cash register.
1 Scales.
1 Small trunk.
1 Wall clock.
1 Phonograph with exercise record.
1 Cot, blanket, sheet and pillow.

HAND PROPS.

Holster, belt and revolver.
Market basket full of groceries.
Photographs, Silver Screen magazine, cigars, matches
    and cigarettes.

ACT II—CASTING DIRECTOR'S OFFICE—OUTSIDE
LOT, HOLLYWOOD

Bench
Desk.
Stool.

Kitchen chair.
Letter boxes, letters.
Bill files.
Signs on wall.
Photos in frames.
Photograph.

ACT III—Scene I—On the Lot

Ladies' small writing desk.
Small chairs.
Armchairs.
Small tables.
Medallion.
Candlesticks.
Vases for flowers.
Writing materials on desk.
Bench.
Desk—flat type.
Motion picture camera.
Small platform.
Looking glass.
Book—"Robinson Crusoe."

ACT III—Scene II—Elsewhere on the Lot

Revolver.
Blanket.
Towel.
Bathrobe.
Bench.
2 Cups coffee and 2 sandwiches.
1 Tray.
1 Megaphone.

ACT IV—Scene I—Jeff Baird's Office

Office desk—flat.

1 Armchair.
2 single chairs.
1 Operator's table.
1 Round table, magazines and books.
Pictures on wall.
1 sheet pictures.

ACT IV—Scene II—Merton's Boarding House

2 Wicker tables, round.
2 Wicker armchairs.
1 Wicker single chair.
1 Wicker bookcase.
1 Wicker flower-box.
1 Wicker "what-not."
1 Wicker settee.
1 Mantelpiece.
1 Wall looking-glass.
3 Large pictures on wall.
1 Medallion.
4 Rugs.
Magazines and papers, match safe and matches.
Brick back for mantel.

LIGHT PLOT

ACT I

Grocery Store:
1000 Watt light blue color, to light ext. backing of
    big window and double door right stage.
1000 Watt white on dimmer door L.C.
1000 Watt amber on dimmer door left.
1000 Watt light blue small window left.
Hanging oil lamps R. and L. center.
Oil lamp on counter.

Footlight strip—4 white and 4 ambers.
    1 Circuit white foots.
    1 Circuit amber fots.
    1 Circuit white, first border.
    1 Circuit amber, first border.

CUES:

1st cue—Gashwiler puts out lamp on counter.
2nd cue—Light out in door left on Merton's entrance.
3rd cue—Light out in door left center on Gashwiler's exit.
4th cue—When Merton pulls down shades in big door and window, first border goes out.
5th cue—When Merton puts out hanging lamp, right center, foots go out.
6th cue—When Merton puts out hanging lamp, left center and light strip in foots go out.
Moonlight coming through small window left should cover Merton as he kneels at head of bed for prayers.

CURTAIN

ACT II—Casting Office

1000 Watt white door light.
1000 Watt white window right center R.C.
5 light strip, white door center C.
5 light strip, white big door, left.
1000 Watt white to light glass backing of big door left. A telephone.
Foots—white and amber, 1st border white and amber. Straight lighting.

ACT III

Back wall and roof of set represents glass studio.

Ten 1000 Watt hanging and six 1000 Watt on floor
to light up back of set.   White.
A—Right and left of small set Cooper-Hewitt Banks.
B—Right and left of small set arc lights.
C—Switchboard.
D—Platform with 2 Arc on top.
X—Three two-light Brackets—not practical.
Foots 1st and 2nd borders—White and amber.

CUES:

Take them from Rosenblatt.

ACT III—Scene II

Blue foots—3 Light strip in foots, left of center.
Amber.
Rain pipe, X—lamp post.   Spotlight.
3 spots to light rain.

ACT IV—Scene I

White and amber foots and 1st border same.

ACT IV—Scene II

White and amber foots and 1st border same.
Telephone, table lamp, floor lamp.

NOTES ON THE SIMPLIFICATION OF THE SETTINGS

The stage directions in this printed copy describe the settings, furniture and props used in the professional production of the play. They are here reprinted in order to enable the amateur producer to understand what the stage looks like. However, it will be found that the simplest sort of sets, furniture and props can be made to furnish a sufficiently suitable background. The essential thing is either a set of screens, three or four of them made in three sections each, or else a very simple interior setting, as any stock theater has, or which may be rented for the occasion.

Acts I* and II require simply an ordinary set, or else three or four of the above-mentioned screens. Act II might even be played before a drop, in which is cut a hole for the window.

Act III, Scene I, can be very simply set. Two parts of the interior set, or else two screens, set according to the directions, are all that is necessary for the setting. The cameraman's outfit can be suggested by an ordinary tripod with a camera on it, else a small box painted to represent a motion-picture camera.

Act III, Scene II, calls for a boat, or part of a

Bolts of goods and dummies can doubtless be borrowed from local drygoods stores, but, if not, can easily be arranged by covering boxes or bundles with various colored cloths; the dummies can be made on a simple wooden framework.

boat, but inasmuch as this is not positively required, and the lines are quite as intelligible if the boat is assumed as being off-stage at the back, no boat need be visible. This scene need have nothing except a drop at the back or anything else that will serve to screen the back of the stage. This is especially easy, as this is a night scene and only the artificial lights from the side of the stage, which can be directed upon one spot, are visible to the audience.

Act IV, Scene I, is a severely plain set. The same interior or screens used in Acts I and II may be used here.

Act IV, Scene II. Same as Act IV, Scene I, regarding the use of scenery.

Merton of the Movies is not a difficult play to set if the producer will bear in mind that only the essentials need be utilized. His endeavor should be to reconstruct only so much background as will allow the action to take place naturally.

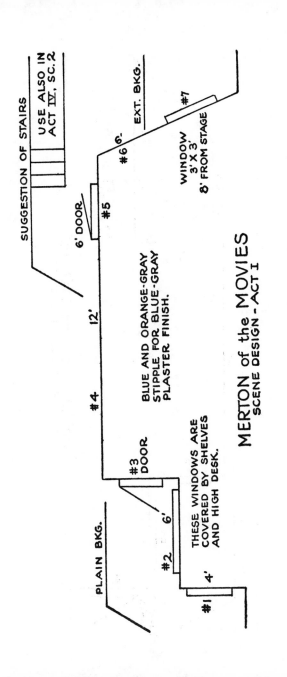

MERTON of the MOVIES
SCENE DESIGN - ACT I

SUGGESTION OF STAIRS

USE ALSO IN ACT IV, SC. 2

EXT. BKG.

6' DOOR

#5

#6

6'

#7

WINDOW
3' X 3'
8' FROM STAGE

12'

#4

BLUE AND ORANGE-GRAY
STIPPLE FOR BLUE-GRAY
PLASTER FINISH.

#3
DOOR

6'

THESE WINDOWS ARE
COVERED BY SHELVES
AND HIGH DESK.

#2

4'

#1

PLAIN BKG.

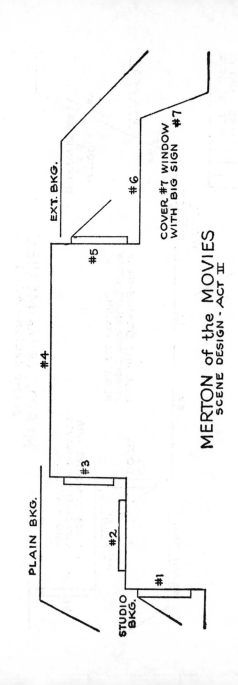

MERTON of the MOVIES
SCENE DESIGN - ACT II

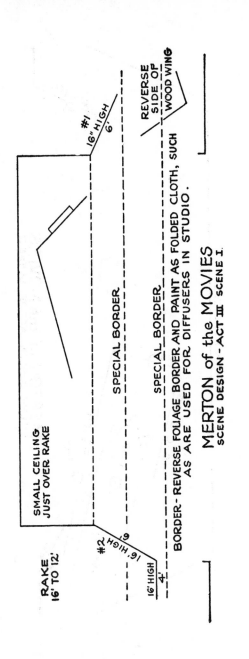

MERTON of the MOVIES
SCENE DESIGN - ACT III SCENE I.

RAKE
16' TO 12'

SMALL CEILING
JUST OVER RAKE

#2
6'
16" HIGH

#1
16" HIGH
6'

SPECIAL BORDER

SPECIAL BORDER

16" HIGH
4'

REVERSE
SIDE OF
WOOD WING

BORDER - REVERSE FOLIAGE BORDER AND PAINT AS FOLDED CLOTH, SUCH
AS ARE USED FOR DIFFUSERS IN STUDIO.

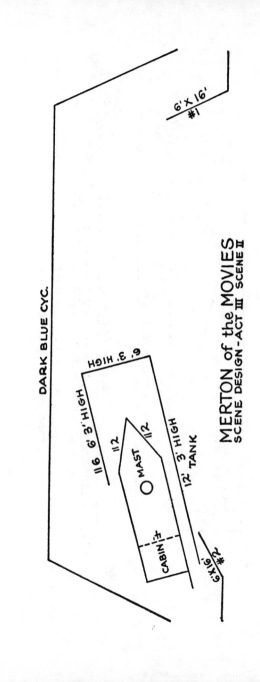

DARK BLUE CYC.

6' X 16'
#1

6' 3' HIGH

116 6' 3' HIGH

112

112

MAST

12' 3' HIGH
TANK

CABIN

6'X16'
#2

MERTON of the MOVIES
SCENE DESIGN—ACT III SCENE II

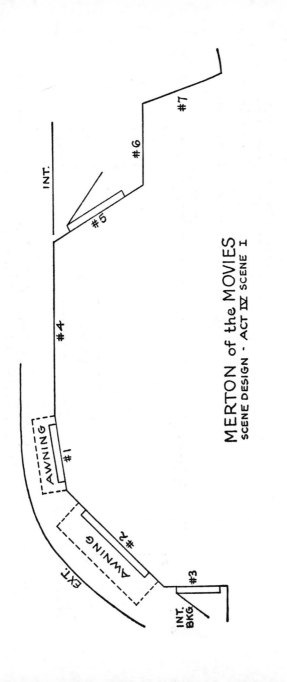

MERTON of the MOVIES
SCENE DESIGN - ACT IV SCENE I

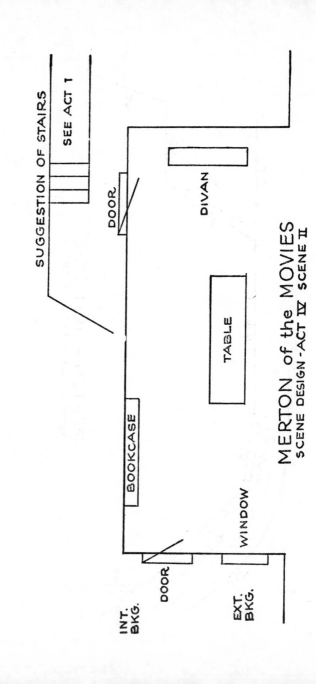

MERTON of the MOVIES
SCENE DESIGN - ACT IV SCENE II

HOME-BUILT

Lighting Equipment
for The Small Stage
By THEODORE FUCHS

This volume presents a series of fourteen simplified designs for building various types of stage lighting and control equipment, with but one purpose in mind—to enable the amateur producer to acquire a complete set of stage lighting equipment at the lowest possible cost. The volume is 8½" x 11" in size, with heavy paper and spiral binding—features which make the volume well suited to practical workshop use.

Community Theatre
A MANUAL FOR SUCCESS
By JOHN WRAY YOUNG

The ideal text for anyone interested in participating in Community Theatre as a vocation or avocation. "Organizing a Community Theatre," "A Flight Plan for the Early Years," "Programming for People—Not Computers," and other chapters are blueprints for solid growth. "Technical, Business and Legal Procedures" cuts a safe and solvent path through some tricky undergrowth. Essential to the library of all community theatres, and to the schools who will supply them with talent in the years to come.

A Breeze from The Gulf

MART CROWLEY
(Little Theatre) Drama

The author of "The Boys in the Band" takes us on a journey back to a small Mississippi town to watch a 15-year-old boy suffer through adolescence to adulthood and success as a writer. His mother is a frilly southern doll who has nothing to fall back on when her beauty fades. She develops headaches and other physical problems, while the asthmatic son turns to dolls and toys at an age when other boys are turning to sports. The traveling father becomes withdrawn, takes to drink; and mother takes to drugs to kill the pain of the remembrances of things past. She eventually ends in an asylum, and the father in his fumbling way tries to tell the son to live the life he must.

> "The boy is plunged into a world of suffering he didn't create. . . . One of the most electrifying plays I've seen in the past few years . . . Scenes boil and hiss . . . The dialogue goes straight to the heart." Reed, Sunday News.

Royalty, $50–$35

ECHOES

N. RICHARD NASH
(All Groups) Drama
2 Men, 1 Woman, Interior

A young man and woman build a low-keyed paradise of happiness within an asylum, only to have it shattered by the intrusion of the outside world. The two characters search, at times agonizingly to determine the difference between illusion and reality. The effort is lightened at times by moments of shared love and "pretend" games, like decorating Christmas trees that are not really there. The theme of love, vulnerable to the surveillances of the asylum, and the ministrations of the psychiatrist, (a non-speaking part) seems as fragile in the constrained setting as it often is in the outside world.

> ". . . even with the tragic, sombre theme there is a note of hope and possible release and the situations presented specifically also have universal applications to give it strong effect . . . intellectual, but charged with emotion."—Reed.

Royalty, $50–$35

VERONICA'S ROOM
IRA LEVIN
(Little Theatre) Mystery
2 Men, 2 Women, Interior

VERONICA'S ROOM is, in the words of one reviewer, "a chew-up-your-finger-nails thriller-chiller" in which "reality and fantasy are entwined in a totally absorbing spider web of who's-doing-what-to-whom." The heroine of the play is 20-year-old Susan Kerner, a Boston University student who, while dining in a restaurant with Larry Eastwood, a young lawyer, is accosted by a charming elderly Irish couple, Maureen and John Mackey (played on Broadway by Eileen Heckart and Arthur Kennedy). These two are overwhelmed by Susan's almost identical resemblance to Veronica Brabissant, a long-dead daughter of the family for whom they work. Susan and Larry accompany the Mackeys to the Brabissant mansion to see a picture of Veronica, and there, in Veronica's room, which has been preserved as a shrine to her memory, Susan is induced to impersonate Veronica for a few minutes in order to solace the only surviving Brabissant, Veronica's addled sister who lives in the past and believes that Veronica is alive and angry with her. "Just say you're not angry with her," Mrs. Mackey instructs Susan. "It'll be such a blessin' for her!" But once Susan is dressed in Veronica's clothes, and Larry has been escorted downstairs by the Mackeys, Susan finds herself locked in the room and locked in the role of Veronica. Or is she really Veronica, in the year 1935, pretending to be an imaginary Susan?

> The play's twists and turns are, in the words of another critic, "like finding yourself trapped in someone else's nightmare," and "the climax is as jarring as it is surprising." "Neat and elegant thriller."—*Village Voice.*

ROYALTY, $50-$35

MY FAT FRIEND
CHARLES LAURENCE
(Little Theatre) Comedy
3 Men, 1 Woman, Interior

Vicky, who runs a bookshop in Hampstead, is a heavyweight. Inevitably she suffers, good-humouredly enough, the slings and arrows of the two characters who share the flat over the shop; a somewhat glum Scottish youth who works in an au pair capacity, and her lodger, a not-so-young homosexual. When a customer—a handsome bronzed man of thirty—seems attracted to her she resolves she will slim by hook or by crook. Aided by her two friends, hard exercise, diet and a graph, she manages to reduce to a stream-lined version of her former self—only to find that it was her rotundity that attracted the handsome book-buyer in the first place. When, on his return, he finds himself confronted by a sylph his disappointment is only too apparent. The newly slim Vicky is left alone once more, to be consoled (up to a point) by her effeminate lodger.

> "My fat Friend is abundant with laughs."—*Times Newsmagazine.* "If you want to laugh go."—*WCBS-TV.*

ROYALTY, $50-$35

PROMENADE, ALL!
DAVID V. ROBISON

(Little Theatre) Comedy
3 Men, 1 Woman, Interior

Four actors play four successive generations of the same family, as their business grows from manufacturing buttons to a conglomerate of international proportions (in the U.S. their perfume will be called Belle Nuit; but in Paris, Enchanted Evening). The Broadway cast included Richard Backus, Anne Jackson, Eli Wallach and Hume Cronyn. Miss Jackson performed as either mother or grandmother, as called for; and Cronyn and Wallach alternated as fathers and grandfathers; with Backus playing all the roles of youth. There are some excellent cameos to perform, such as the puritanical mother reading the Bible to her son without realizing the sexual innuendoes; or the 90-year-old patriarch who is agreeable to trying an experiment in sexology but is afraid of a heart attack.

> "So likeable; jolly and splendidly performed."—*N.Y. Daily News.* "The author has the ability to write amusing lines, and there are many of them."—*N.Y. Post.* "Gives strong, lively actors a chance for some healthy exercise. And what a time they have at it!"—*CBS-TV.*

ROYALTY, $50-$35

ACCOMMODATIONS
NICK HALL

(Little Theatre) Comedy
2 Men, 2 Women, Interior

Lee Schallert, housewife, feeling she may be missing out on something, leaves her husband, Bob, and her suburban home and moves into a two-room Greenwich Village apartment with two roommates. One roommate, Pat, is an aspiring actress, never out of characters or costumes, but, through an agency mix up, the other roommate is a serious, young, graduate student—male. The ensuing complications make a hysterical evening.

> "An amusing study of marital and human relations . . . a gem . . . It ranks as one of the funniest ever staged."—*Labor Herald.* "The audience at Limestone Valley Dinner Theater laughed at "Accommodations" until it hurt.—*News American.* "Superior theater, frivolous, perhaps, but nonetheless superior. It is light comedy at its best."—*The Sun, Baltimore.*

ROYALTY, $50-$25

THE GOOD DOCTOR

NEIL SIMON

(All Groups) Comedy

2 Men, 3 Women. Various settings.

With Christopher Plummer in the role of the Writer, we are introduced to a composite of Neil Simon and Anton Chekhov, from whose short stories Simon adapted the capital vignettes of this collection. Frances Sternhagen played, among other parts, that of a harridan who storms a bank and upbraids the manager for his gout and lack of money. A father takes his son to a house where he will be initiated into the mysteries of sex, only to relent at the last moment, and leave the boy more perplexed than ever. In another sketch a crafty seducer goes to work on a wedded woman, only to realize that the woman has been in command from the first overture. Let us not forget the classic tale of a man who offers to drown himself for three rubles. The stories are droll, the portraits affectionate, the humor infectious, and the fun unending.

> "As smoothly polished a piece of work as we're likely to see all season."—*N.Y. Daily News.* "A great deal of warmth and humor —vaudevillian humor—in his retelling of these Chekhovian tales."—*Newhouse Newspapers.* "There is much fun here . . . Mr. Simon's comic fancy is admirable."—*N.Y. Times.*

(Music available. Write for particulars.)
ROYALTY, $50-$35

The Prisoner of Second Avenue

NEIL SIMON

(All Groups) Comedy

2 Men, 4 Women, Interior

Mel is a well-paid executive of a fancy New York company which has suddenly hit the skids and started to pare the payroll. Anxiety doesn't help; Mel, too, gets the ax. His wife takes a job to tide them over, then she too is sacked. As if this weren't enough, Mel is fighting a losing battle with the very environs of life. Polluted air is killing everything that grows on his terrace; the walls of the high-rise apartment are paper-thin, so that the private lives of a pair of German stewardesses next door are open books to him; the apartment is burgled; and his psychiatrist dies with $23,000 of his money. Mel does the only thing left for him to do: he has a nervous breakdown. It is on recovery that we come to esteem him all the more. For Mel and his wife and people like them have the resilience, the grit to survive.

> "Now all this, mind you, is presented primarily in humorous terms."—*N.Y. Daily News.* "A gift for taking a grave subject and, without losing sight of its basic seriousness, treating it with hearty but sympathetic humor . . . A talent for writing a wonderfully funny line . . . full of humor and intelligence . . . Fine fun."—*N.Y. Post.* "Creates an atmosphere of casual cataclysm, and everyday urban purgatory of copelessness from which laughter seems to be released like vapor from the city's manholes."—*Time.*

ROYALTY, $50-$35

A COMMUNITY OF TWO

JEROME CHODOROV

(All Groups) Comedy

4 Men, 3 Women, Interior

Winner of a Tony Award for "Wonderful Town." Co-author of "My Sister Eileen," "Junior Miss," "Anniversary Waltz." This is a charming off-beat comedy about Alix Carpenter, a fortyish divorceè of one month who has been locked out of her own apartment and is rescued by her thrice-divorced neighbor across the hall, Michael Jardeen. During the course of the two hours in which it takes to play out the events of the evening, we meet Alix's ex-husband, a stuffed shirt from Wall Street, her son, who has run away from prep school with his girl, heading for New Mexico and a commune. Michael's current girl friend, Olga, a lady anthropologist just back from Lapland, and Mr. Greenberg, a philosopher-locksmith. All take part in the hilarious doings during a blizzard that rages outside the building and effects everybody's lives. But most of all, and especially, we get to know the eccentric Michael Jardeen, and the confused and charming Alix Carpenter, who discover that love might easily happen, even on a landing, in the course of a couple of hours of highstress living.

> "Thoroughly delightful comedy."—*St. Louis-Post Dispatch.* "A joy."—*Cleveland Plain Dealer.* "Skillful fun by Jerome Chodorov."—*Toronto Globe Star.*

ROYALTY, $50-$35

ROMAN CONQUEST

JOHN PATRICK

(All Groups) Comedy

One set—3 Women, 6 Men

The romantic love story of two American girls living in the romantic city of Rome in a romantic garret at the foot of the famous Spanish steps. One of the world's richest young women takes her less fortunate girl friend to Italy to hide unknown and escape notoriety while she attempts to discover if she has any talent as an artist—free of position and prestige. Their misadventures with language and people supply a delightful evening of pure entertainment. Remember the movies "Three Coins in the Fountain" and "Love Is A Many Splendored Thing"? This new comedy is in the same vein by the same Pulitzer Prize winning playwright.

ROYALTY, $50-$35

COUNT DRACULA

TED TILLER

(All Groups) Mystery comedy
7 Men, 2 Women. Interior with Small Inset
1930 Costumes (optional)

Based on Bram Stoker's 19th Century novel, "Dracula." This is a new, witty version of the classic story of a suave vampire whose passion is sinking his teeth into the throats of beautiful young women. Mina, his latest victim, is the ward of Dr. Seward in whose provincial insane asylum the terrifying action transpires. Her finance arrives from London, worried over her strange inertia and trance-like state. Equally concerned is Professor Van Helsing, specialist in rare maladies, who senses the supernatural at work. Added trouble comes from Sybil, Dr. Sewards demented, sherry-tippling sister and from Renfield, a schizophrenic inmate in league with the vampire. But how to trap this ghoul who can transform himself into a bat, materialize from fog, dissolve in mist? There are many surprising but uncomplicated stage effects, mysterious disappearances, secret panels, howling wolves, bats that fly over the audience, an unexpected murder, and magic tricks which include Dracula's vanishing in full view of the spectators.

> Despite much gore, ". . . the play abounds with funny lines. There is nothing in it but entertainment."—*Springfield, Mass. News.*

ROYALTY, $50-$25

FRANKENSTEIN

TIM KELLY

(All Groups)
4 Men, 4 Women, Interior

Victor Frankenstein, a brilliant young scientist, returns to his chateau on the shores of Lake Geneva to escape some terrible pursuer. No one can shake free the dark secret that terrifies him. Not his mother, nor his financee Elizabeth, nor his best friend, Henry Clerval. Even the pleading of a gypsy girl accused of murdering Victor's younger brother falls on deaf ears, for Victor has brought into being a "Creature" made from bits and pieces of the dead! The Creature tracks Victor to his sanctuary to demand a bride to share its loneliness—one as wretched as the Creature itself. Against his better judgment, Victor agrees and soon the household is invaded by murder, despair and terror! The play opens on the wedding night of Victor and Elizabeth, the very time the Creature has sworn to kill the scientist for destroying its intended mate, and ends, weeks later, in a horrific climax of dramatic suspense! In between there is enough macabre humor to relieve the mounting tension. Perhaps the truest adaptation of Mary Shelley's classic yet. Simple to stage and a guaranteed audience pleaser.

ROYALTY, $25.00

The Tandem Library

A Selection of 20 Plays from

All in the Family

Sanford and Son

Good Times

Maude

For details of titles available and royalty fees apply to Samuel French, Inc.

The Happy Hunter

(ALL GROUPS)
Comedy—CHARLES FEYDEAU

English Adaptation by Barnett Shaw
7 Men, 3 Women—2 Interiors

Chandel tells Yvonne he is going hunting with Castillo, but when Castillo turns up unexpectedly, she sees the hoax, and therefore decides to yield to Roussel's amorous advances, going to his bachelor den with him. But, across the hall, Chandel is having a rendezvous with Madame Castillo. A hectic evening ensues, complicated by an eccentric landlady and by the appearance of Yvonne's nephew, whose girl friend used to live there. The police, seeking Madame Castillo's lover, grab Roussel, while Chandel escapes through the window and runs off with Roussel's trousers. The mix-up unravels in act three, with one surprise after the. other, Yvonne winning all tricks while her husband gets the punishment.

ROYALTY, $35-$25

A Gown for His Mistress

(Little Theatre) Farce
GEORGE FEYDEAU

English Translation by Barnett Shaw
4 Men, 6 Females—Interior
Can be played 1900 Period or Chic Modern

A wild and saucy matrimonial mix-up by the celebrated author of A FLEA IN HER EAR.

Dr. Moulineaux stays out all night after a futile attempt to meet his mistress, Suzanne, at the Opera Ball. He tells his wife he has been up all night with a friend, Bassinet, who is near death, but at that moment Bassinet walks in. Upbraided by his mother-in-law for his infidelity, he decides he must no longer allow Suzanne to pretend to be a patient. For a hide-away, he rents an apartment that formerly belonged to a dressmaker. In Act II he is courting Suzanne in his new apartment when her husband walks in. Posing as a dressmaker he gets rid of the husband momentarily, but is caught in a desperate entanglement when his wife, his mother-in-law, Bassinet, and Bassinet's wife appear. In Act III, Moulineaux's household is in an uproar but he manages to lie his way out of it all with the help of Bassinet who has a photograph that seems to solve everything. Outstanding male and female roles. The play moves rapidly and is an excellent work-out for alert actors and actresses.

ROYALTY, $35-$25

HANDBOOK

for

THEATRICAL APPRENTICES
By Dorothy Lee Tompkins

Here is a common sense book on theatre, fittingly sub-titled, "A Practical Guide in All Phases of Theatre." Miss Tompkins has wisely left art to the artists and written a book which deals only with the practical side of the theatre. All the jobs of the theatre are categorized, from the star to the person who sells soft drinks at intermission. Each job is defined, and its basic responsibilities given in detail. An invaluable manual for every theatre group in explaining to novices the duties of apprenticeship, and in reassessing its own organizational structure and functions.

"If you are an apprentice or are just aspiring in any capacity, then you'll want to read and own Dorothy Lee Tompkins' A HANDBOOK FOR THEATRICAL APPRENTICES. It should be required reading for any drama student anywhere and is a natural for the amateur in any phase of the theatre."—George Freedley, Morning Telegraph.

"It would be helpful if the HANDBOOK FOR THEATRICAL APPRENTICES were in school or theatrical library to be used during each production as a guide to all participants."—Florence E. Hill, Dramatics Magazine.